Mitāhara

FOOD WISDOM FROM MY INDIAN KITCHEN

Mitāhāra

FOOD WISDOM FROM MY INDIAN KITCHEN

RUJUTA DIWEKAR

Contents

FOREWORD	6
INTRODUCTION	8
A book of recipes	10
WINTER	28
The season of togetherness	30
Amla–ginger sherbet	46
Til gul	48
Kothimbir wadi	50
Navalkol koshimbir	52
Sheng amti	53
Vangi bhaat	56
Bajra raab	58
Thalipeeth and loni	60
Bajra–green lahasun laddoo	64
Bhogichi bhaji	66
Chivda	68
Chhole	70
SUMMER	72
The season of simplicity	74
Variyali sherbet	98
Mango milkshake	100

Dahi poha	101
White onion koshimbir	104
Curd rice and lemon pickle	105
Khichdi and date raita	110
Lauki sabzi, jowar roti with ghee, and peanut chutney	114
Kokum saar	118
Aam ras and puri	122
Ole kaju usal	124
Banana halwa	126
Vaal usal	127
Ragi kheer	130

RAINS — 132
The season of sustainability — 134

Rice pej	146
Ragi laddoo	148
Sabudana wada and chutney	152
Curry leaves chutney	154
White corn in kadhi and rice	158
Masala bhaat and yam kaap	162
Danyachi amti and vari tandul	166
Ukadiche modak	168
Narali bhaat	170
Shewla bhaji	174
Alu wadi	178
Ambadi bhaji	180

CHANGE OF SEASONS — 182
The period of fasting and feasting — 184

Kulith kalan	202
Aliv laddoo	204
Upvasache thalipeeth	206
Mango pickle	207
Dal and bhaat	210
Amboli	212
Pithla and bhakri	214
Ambe dal	218
Banana flower sabzi	220
White pumpkin halwa	222
Rava–nariyal laddoo	224
Shrikhand	226
Kantola vegetable	228
Besan cheela	229

Glossary	230
Index	234
Acknowledgments	238
Imprints	240

Foreword

They say the way to a man's heart is through his stomach, but I have come to realize that the way to a man's growth is through his kitchen.

My mother raised me and my brother with our feet on the ground and chores in the kitchen – a recipe for happiness, she would say. I always thought she was being difficult, but now that I am over 30, married, and a father, I finally understand what she meant.

Making meals is a bit like making movies – an act of love, courage, and above all, risk. But then, *risk hai tabhi toh ishq hai* (love is a risky affair). When you enter the kitchen, the world stops existing, *waqt tham jaata hai* (time comes to a halt), and all that matters is your attention to cooking. That is all a simple khichdi demands of you, and the same goes for an omelet or puran poli. Attention to detail is everything, and learning to cook is a great way to master it. A movie or a meal, made with love, is a success even before it is watched or savoured. The process is the true joy.

Cooking at home is also a delicious way to stay healthy. I will not lie – being an actor, looking a certain way is an occupational hazard for me. It is easy to get carried away with trends and quick fixes. But with age and experience, you learn that the only foolproof way to fuel your dreams and aspirations – and avoid injury or disillusionment – is to keep it simple and eat home-cooked food. It is a great leveller too. Whether you have had a bad day at work or a great one, whether your last movie was a hit or a flop, a homemade meal welcomes you in its embrace with open arms.

Luckily for me, food is a big part of movie sets, and coming together over lunch is an integral part of moviemaking. Sets with good food are always fun to work on. My wife, Natasha, is a foodie too. Pithla with bhakri or dahi rice, she eats everything with the same zest she has for life. A partner who shows no *nakhra* (fuss) with food is the biggest green flag. A woman who can eat her favourite food without fear is the woman who will see you through your bad times. This is Rujuta's relationship mantra, one she shared with me even though I never asked for it. But, she is my speed dial whenever I am confused or conflicted about what to eat.

As she says, food is the most delicious and beautiful expression of love. This book is a love letter to home-cooked food, a wonderful collection of wisdom and recipes, complemented by her signature wit and some delicious pictures of her famous food plates. I am sure you will have as much fun going through the pages as you will cooking and eating the recipes inside.

For me, now that I have a daughter, I look forward to making a steaming bowl of dal chawal for her and listening to her yap away about her school gossip on a rainy day. No matter what each of us does in our lives, food, family, and the ability to share meals, memories, and movies with one another is what makes us human.

Long live diversity, long live dal chawal.

Varun Dhawan, *Indian actor*
Mumbai, November 2024

INTRODUCTION

A book of recipes

In 2009, as soon as my first book, *Don't Lose Your Mind, Lose Your Weight*, crossed 50,000 in sales, my editor called me and said, "Now you must write a recipe book".

"No chance," I told her.

"But why not?" she argued back. "Every bestselling weight-loss book goes with a recipe book. Don't write it right away; let's look at a 2010 release."

"I don't want anyone eating for weight loss," I replied. "I want people to eat for love, to nurture themselves, and develop a sense of belonging. I may have a bestseller under my belt, but my feet are still on the ground. How could I possibly write a book that covers the diversity of Indian cooking, the wisdom of its women, the centrality of its kitchens? And don't forget, I don't even cook." The conversation ended there.

Fast forward to 2022, just a dozen years later, but the world had changed in many ways. Social media scrolling has become everyone's pastime and everything is becoming polarized, even food opinions. The pandemic happened and we are now in the post-pandemic world, in a suspended sort of reality, one that seems to write its script like an episode of the futuristic web series *Black Mirror*. Khichdi, arguably India's go-to dish for a no-fuss meal, which is easy to cook and light on the stomach, turned into the most ordered dish on food delivery apps during the COVID-19 pandemic. People seemed to want a home-cooked meal, but did not know how to make it. If you did know how to cook it, it would be ready 10 minutes faster than the quickest delivery service, and yummier and healthier.

Somewhere in this suspended reality, I met Aparna Sharma, the then managing director of Dorling Kindersley India, and she asked me to write a recipe book. Our eyes locked and I said yes. By this time, I was older and, dare I say, more mature. I had also cooked endlessly during the pandemic – it was my newfound love.

12   MITĀHĀRA

Winter produce from the farm

INTRODUCTION 13

Home food thali

Actually, cooking had been in my heart for a long time. I just never acted on it. I had, in the past, cooked food. But during the pandemic, it became therapeutic and I woke up every day longing to cook more. My kitchen changed, as did my perspective and my social media posts, but most importantly, my life changed. I realize now that cooking is like love, at once complicated and simple. The romance, the meaning, the nurturing comes out of this paradox. And like love, cooking must touch everyone's lives, hence this book.

Woh kya hai ki strategy se sirf profit badhtay hai, pyar nahi. Pyar ke liye khana aur khilana, khane wala aur khilane wala dono kaabil chahiye. (Strategy can only increase profit, not love. For love, food and the process of making that food, the one eating it and the one cooking the food, both should be worthy.)

If you asked me about the most attractive trait in a man, I would say it is his ability to pay attention. With time, everything fades – success, money, and looks, but it is the attentiveness that stays. Cooking is the celebration of this human quality of attentiveness, of the humility and confidence to pay attention even if you are making a dal for the thousandth time in your life.

It is like what a dear client and one of the most sought-after cardiologists from the Apollo Group, Dr Sai Satish, once told me. He said that he tells every doctor he trains: "It does not matter if this is your 40th or 400th surgery, you must remember that, for your patient, this is their only heart. He is the only husband of his wife, the only father of his child. If you do not treat it with the same attention as your first surgery, you are doing this wrong".

Great artists will tell you the same thing. Chintan Upadhyay, a young, promising Dhrupad singer, once told me that he practises his music every day. He said, "Sometimes, the *sa* [the first note of the scale] feels so beautiful that I cannot help but wonder, 'Where did this come from?' Other times, even when I give it my best, I only hit an average note. However, in life, once you realize that something far greater is with you – once you truly understand and feel that music is greater than the musician, and that art is greater than the artist – you can sing without worry. You feel light, regardless of success or failure. You feel gratitude for the joy of the

practice itself, and no matter what happens, you know you will practise again tomorrow." Cooking is exactly like that. Every day is a new day in the kitchen. Every day, it is the same dal or the same rice, but it is new. Our recipes are the legacies that keep us ageless and fresh – even alive – long after we are gone. The best thing you can do is eat it with the same attention that you gave to cooking it.

Through this book, I intend to take you on a journey to unravel the mystery behind our love, almost obsession, for cooking. I hope to bring to the fore the unifying principles of love, nurture, and the sense of belonging that we express through our diverse cooking that varies according to seasons. This is how India celebrates life, this is how it overcomes petty squabbles at home, this is how we live together as an eclectic mix of communities. It is through food, through cooking, and through sharing that we live and leave legacies behind.

The secret to a light kitchen

Once my friend, the Hindi film actor Varun Dhawan, was over for lunch with his wife Natasha and his mother Lally, who is also one of my earliest clients. They had come over for puran poli (sweet stuffed flatbread), but got pithla and bhakri (a savoury gram flour curry and flatbread) instead, and they loved it.

"You know these actors, they will come for lunch, but bring their own food," Lally ragged Varun.

"Come on, Mom! Why would I do that at Rujuta's?" replied Varun, "Her food is very light but still very good. I do not know how she does it."

"By making it in my kitchen, Varun," I said.

We had this healthy banter going all afternoon and after they left, I started thinking about my kitchen. I love my kitchen, of course, but what makes it so special? I recalled Varun saying "People do make food in their own kitchen, but it is usually quite rich".

I realized then that my kitchen was special because I am a fourth-generation working woman in my family. My mother, her mother, her mother's mother, all had full-time jobs. So, while they cooked and nurtured their families, they kept meals light. Life is already heavy for working women so it is best to avoid heavy meals. Nothing "rich" for working women who lead full-time lives outside their homes.

INTRODUCTION 15

Banana flower and fruit

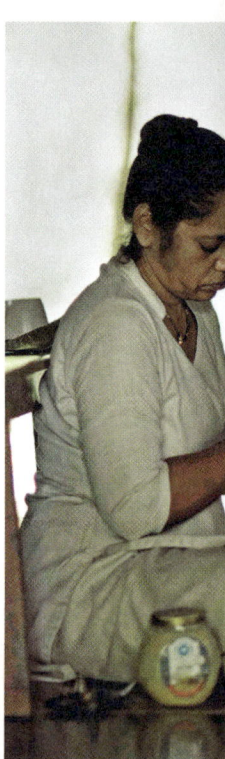

This is in contrast to what one sees in cooking videos on social media platforms. It means that we keep almost nothing "prepared" or ready-to-use in the fridge.

Let me share my secret to keeping things light in the kitchen. The idea is to keep the main ingredient as the main ingredient. It is to remember that you run a home, not a restaurant; that dessert can be made with just jaiphal (nutmeg) or elaichi (cardamom). You do not need both. It is to remember that *teekha* (spicy) can come from either green chilli or kali mirch (black pepper), you do not need both. It is to realize that you can garnish with either coconut or fresh coriander. It's often said that every great film is first created at the writing table, during the scripting process, and then at the editing table. The actors, their performances, and publicity cannot make up for a weak foundation. So, treat this book like a script. What you leave out while cooking is the editing – whether you make it yourself or delegate it to your cook wouldn't make much difference.

If the phrase "less is more" holds true anywhere, it is in the kitchen. Cooking can be a breeze if you let go of the checklist, food pictures, or recipe. If you did not remember to put in an ingredient, it probably

The kitchen and farming team

was not important to begin with. Allow this book to be your framework. Then take over, put yourself in the dish and, only then can you truly own it.

I use this concept in my first line of work too – diets. When I start working with people, I share many hacks with them, whether it is about holidays, late lunches, or late night cravings. Then, one day, they share their secrets with me – how they managed their holiday or something that went on endlessly and delayed lunch. They tell me my hack like it is their discovery, their idea. And that is when I know that I have done a good job. If they own it, they will rock it.

A beautiful kitchen just needs one thing: for you to use it 30 minutes a day and it will glow all day long. Just like workouts, you do not need much – 30 minutes a day, 150 minutes a week, and you prevent diseases, live longer, and look sexier. Just like how you need to spread out your workouts between strength, stamina, stability, and stretching, you need to spread out that grand kitchen entry too.

Here are five signs that you have a beautiful kitchen. Even checking three would be very good.

• At least one ingredient that you consume daily (this can not be tea or coffee) is single origin. It could be the rajma (kidney beans) from the mountains of Kashmir or Himachal Pradesh, rice from your ancestral village, or lentils from the farmers' market.

• The silverware that your family, your mother, grandmother, or aunt gave you is in use in your kitchen and not in your bank locker. You could be drinking water in it, using it to serve the dal hot, or even eating dinner in it.

• The dark corner of your kitchen has a bowl of fresh, dahi (curd), kept there to set. I understand that only those living in India or buying fresh milk abroad can afford to do this. But if you do, then you are already tweaking the settings based on the season. You are already being intelligent. Hurray!

• You may have heard of "tablescaping". Long before this, Indian women "kitchenscaped", that is, arranged things in a way where they needed them. A kitchen is beautiful when the placement or design of at least a few things in it is according to an elderly woman in the family. It could be your grandmother, grandaunt, an ageing neighbour or even a household cook or hired chef. Just like there is divinity in detail, there's beauty in efficiency.

• Contribution from every member of the family – it could be something as simple as the children putting their plates back in the kitchen, the spouse cooking a khichdi, or a guest who teaches you a trick or two – basically an accessible and equitable kitchen. A rich kitchen has daily footfalls of its own family and friends. That is how it stays in the business of keeping everyone healthy.

• Here is an extra one, perhaps not possible for those in cities such as Mumbai – a quiet corner to sit and sip or chew on your own thoughts. If you have all of the above, you have really made it. For the rest of us, we shall overcome one day.

A collective wisdom

A few years ago, I visited the Narayan Koti complex, a cluster of ancient temples located in a beautiful valley near Kedarnath, in Uttarakhand. The guide explained that the temples came into existence because of the Pandavas. "*Pandavo ne banaye the* (the Pandavas built them)," he said. In the Sanskrit epic *Mahabharata*, Yudhishthira, Bhima, Arjuna, Nakula, and Sahadeva are five brothers collectively referred to as Pandavas, the sons of the king Pandu. In India, when no one really knows who built a temple, when it is not the charity or the order of some kingdom or a king, when it is the collective effort of people, it is common to attribute it to the Pandavas. *Woh Nakula hai ya Bhima hai, maloom nahi, lekin jaise har ek ungli muthi ki takat banti hai, waise har ghar, har parivar ke contribution se yeh bane hai* (no one knows if it is Nakula or Bhima. But just as every finger contributes to the strength of a fist, every household, every family has made these possible.)

A variety of local pulses

Indian food is pretty much the same. The recipes do not belong to one chef, one kitchen, or even one ingredient, but they are built by constant innovations, small and big contributions, by mothers and grandmothers who ruled over and toiled in the kitchen, who kept not just the fires and food warm but even our hearts. And what better way to pay an ode to them than to cook just like them. Just a little bit like them at least. Therefore, use this book wisely, and remember that the recipes do not make a dish, you make it. More importantly, your fearlessness to give a part of you to it makes the dish.

I have two paintings from Tabo Monastery, the oldest surviving Thangka school, in Spiti Valley, Himachal Pradesh, in my office. One depicts Manjushri, the Buddha of wisdom, and the other, Avalokiteshvara, the Buddha of compassion. "Without both in equal amounts," the lama at Tabo had told me, "you cannot have real power." The power of every dish, too, comes from the mix of wisdom and compassion – wisdom to tweak temperatures, ingredients, and even the style of cooking based on the *ritu* (season) and the compassion to serve, uplift, and contribute without expecting anything in return, let alone credit or recognition.

There truly lies the power of the seemingly simple khichdi, a one-pot dish of rice and pulses. This reminds me of the lyrics of a popular Hindi song "*Jag ghoomeya thaare jaisa na koi*" (I roamed the entire world but I could not find anyone like you). This feeling comes from the fact that the dish carries the wisdom and the compassion of so many who have lived before us.

This book aspires to help you explore the full potential of something as simple as khichdi by cooking it at home and not having it delivered to you from a cloud kitchen. It aims to remind you of the forgotten wisdom of eating in sync with the seasons. The hope is that you will live life to its fullest by celebrating seasons, ingredients, and your kitchen, while building a robust appetite to devour every experience of life.

Bakul flowers

MITĀHĀRA

Wild and uncultivated veggies

The three appetites

The yogis tell us that we must feed and eat according to three distinct *bhuk* (appetite) – *hita bhuk* (appetite that considers the wellbeing of all), *mita bhuk* (appetite that considers portion sizes so that you feel fulfilled, but not full), and *ritu bhuk* (appetite that considers the season, the wind, the heat, the rain, and the cold). When we eat in accordance with our diverse cuisine and cultures, we take all of these into account. Bharatiya *sabhyata* (civilization) and *sanskriti* (culture) stems from our kitchens. Until not so long ago (and still in some parts of India, especially the Himalayan states), our kitchens were the most critical and central part of our homes. This is where the grand plan to nourish these types of appetites is set into action. It is rooted in the belief that *bhuk marna* (the waning of appetite) is the first sign of life leaving us. The phrase "*khaate peete ghar ka insaan* (from a well-nourished family)" refers to someone who has a zest for life and in whom the wisdom to consider these three variables, before cooking anything at all, is still alive.

A balancing act

Mitahara is the act of eating in balance; to be moderate in one's consumption without denying oneself a good meal. It means paying attention to what one eats, to enjoy the flavour, taste, and texture of local, seasonal, and traditional food.

It borrows from the yogic wisdom of living within our ecological means. It embodies not just respect for diversity in food, but also in people, their cultures and cuisines. In the modern world, the subtlety of eating diverse foods is under serious threat. When diversity is lost, the small joys of sharing meals, of getting to know each other over food is lost.

As you turn the pages, you will find ideas to imbue the joy and spirit of the season with a sherbet, something sweet or savoury, or even a celebratory meal. Some are just regular, daily meals, others are accompaniments or digestive drinks. These will bring diverse nutrients to your plate, flavours to your palate, and a smile to your face. Some will remind you of laughter, some others may get you thinking about a local equivalent in your region or culture.

Groundnuts

Purple and white radish

Over time, you will rediscover the adventure and joy of cooking. It will stoke your creativity and appetite. You will notice that you don't need a lot on your plate, you just need to chew on it, slowly, and satiety will smile upon you.

The point is to create room in your *dil* (heart) and *dimaag* (head) for not just food and cooking, but of life and living. The book will take you through the seasons; it will remind you of forgotten foods and familiar tastes; and it will outline what you could eat for breakfast, lunch, dinner, and in between. I also hope to dispel the myth that Indian cooking is laborious, tedious, or heavy. In fact, it is like the soft breeze of the sea when you have just completed a 5km (3 miles) run. It is like a pat on your back when you were expecting a rap on your knuckles. It is like getting upgraded to first class when you have bought economy tickets. I invite you to flip through the pages and feel the warmth and wisdom of our women whose recipes have stood the test of time.

Happy reading and cooking.

WINTER

At this time, people enjoy the insides of houses whose windows are shut, fire, and sunlight… now, sandalwood, cool as moonrays, doesn't delight the hearts of people.

Kalidasa in *Ritusamhara* on winter, or सर्दी (sardi)

The season of togetherness

Our shastras (scriptures) tell us winter is when everything falls apart only so that it may rise again – newer and better. This is a time of *nidhan* or reflection, to look within, before you can look forward to the vibrant colours and flowers of spring. In this season, the *pind* or body looks and feels most like the *brahmanda* or nature. Everything feels dry and sometimes the chill reaches the bone, which is why it is also the season of all things hot and lubricating. In terms of health, what you eat during winter pretty much decides whether, next year, you emerge in a 2.0 version or a deteriorated avatar.

This is the time of the year when grandmothers complain the most of aches and pains, and when conversations around gas and constipation in families are on the rise. This is also the festive season with heavy meals, late nights, and binge drinking, which do not help the body in any way. But in Indian kitchens, there is a time-tested *upaay* or remedy to help us bear the consequences of all that fun and frolic.

The glow of a community

Festivals are a time for coming together and sharing meals. Much of the experience is rooted in the person who prepares the food, who infuses it with their own special touch. The act of pouring ourselves into the dishes we make becomes second nature during these celebrations. Community meals often have a special significance as they celebrate a particular member's unique skill in making a specific dish. This not only honours the individuals involved, but also acknowledges the season and our capacity to savour and enjoy more.

In Spiti Valley, a mountainous cold desert in Himachal Pradesh, winter temperatures can dip to as low as -30°C (-22°F). However, the region celebrates many festivals during the winter months, with community gatherings, food, and singing. It is a reassurance that even in the harshest conditions, you have your own people and practices to keep you warm.

During these moments of family and community, conversations revolve around shared experiences, of past memories and joyful times, and a wish for the next generation to enjoy a life similar to their own. The food, people, and stories may seem familiar, but there is a sense of freshness and novelty. It is perhaps why we tend to eat more in a community setting than when we are alone. The same meal, when consumed alone, may feel like an overindulgence. In a communal setting, this is driven by enjoyment and a sense of being cared for. During festivals, people pay attention to what they are eating, savour each bite with great love, and eagerly anticipate at least one special dish. These occasions are marked by a mindful appreciation of food.

One of my favourite festive dishes is vangi bhaat (*see pp56–57*), a speciality of the Kokanastha Brahmin community, who hail from Konkan, the coastal region of western India. One could say that it is their version of meat biryani. It features brinjal or aubergine cooked with rice and spices, and is celebrated for its special status during significant occasions. Quick and straightforward to prepare, it reflects the culinary traditions of the community. When vangi bhaat appears on the menu, it often signifies the presence of someone who has learnt this from their *aaji* (grandmother).

Being intuitive

I have often wondered why brinjal is combined with rice in vangi bhaat. There seems to be no technical reason for this combination. Our cooking traditions have developed through observation over time. Our grandmothers understood texture, flavour, and the principles of ingredient combinations better than many modern food scientists. They created dishes without the need for emulsifiers or additives, relying on intuitive knowledge of what works well together. This is how combinations came to be. Their approach was about finding practical solutions that offer both taste and nutrition, while minimizing effort and maximizing efficiency in the kitchen.

The dishes prepared are also meant to cater to a variety of tastes as, in most Indian homes, every meal is shared. That is why there is a careful balance of flavours – sweet alongside something slightly bitter or salty, paired with plain, unseasoned options such as steamed rice. This ensures that there is something for everyone,

Palak puri thali

eliminating the need to cook additional dishes if someone dislikes a particular flavour. Additionally, these combinations consider factors such as ease of chewing and digestion, making sure that every aspect of the meal is thoughtfully addressed. Puran poli (sweet stuffed flatbread) is a great example. It is hard to digest, so is eaten with accompaniments such as ghee or milk, making it digestible. This thoughtful pairing ensures that one can still look forward to enjoying puran poli each year, without being deterred by the difficulty of digesting it. One can substitute or add dishes to meals according to preference as well. So, on its own, puran poli is a complete meal, but when paired with spiced rice, it becomes a special treat.

However, certain dishes can only be had together, such as chhole and bhature (spicy chickpeas and deep-fried bread). Both elements are needed – one without the other is incomplete. Unlike street food combinations, which have strict pairing, home-cooked combinations can be enjoyed separately or together. They are also versatile enough to be packed and sent home with guests, such as palak puri (spinach-flavoured deep-fried bread). These home combinations are designed to be more wholesome and adaptable.

In India, the approach to food has always been more than just about nutrients; its culinary traditions are more pragmatic, inclusive, and enduring. They have always prioritized a balanced approach to food and meals, anticipating long-term needs rather than chasing fleeting trends.

The warmth of a massage

Winter also celebrates the *roop* or form. The cold winter air often leads to the dryness of skin, requiring moisturization and lubrication, which in turn leads to warmth and lustre on the inside. On Diwali, the festival of lights, which often comes at the cusp of winter, my family and I start the day with an oil massage for the whole body. It is the perfect morning ritual for winters, a tradition far older than oil pulling. Til oil and apricot oil dominate here. One could, of course, still use coconut oil for the hair, but enriched with some methi (fenugreek seeds) and curry leaves to get rid of dandruff and to prevent hair loss.

Most Maharashtrians celebrate Diwali with an invigorating oil massage for the body in the morning. This cherished tradition involves applying *ubtan* (an Ayurvedic paste, which is a blend of sandalwood, saffron, and other local ingredients) mixed with oil before taking a long, hot water bath. Families wake up before sunrise and light a lamp while it is still dark. They give themselves and their children a massage with this special mix before bathing. By daybreak, everyone is refreshed and ready in traditional attire to celebrate what is possibly the biggest festival of the year for the Hindus.

Starting the day

Nothing can be more delicious and heart-warming than a winter's breakfast. It is the season of koki and thalipeeth (types of flatbread) with safed makkhan (white butter), but also of poha (flattened rice) with milk and jaggery. To give the kitchen and stomach a break, preparations with dahi, such as dahi churra or dahi poha (versions of flattened rice), or poha with peas are easy alternatives. This is also when kitchens use millets, such as bajra and rajgeera (amaranth), with as much gusto as til and nuts, along with makkhan and dahi. Cooking oils can change as well, shifting to til oil tadka (tempering) from the routine of groundnut, mustard, or coconut oil tadka based on the region you come from.

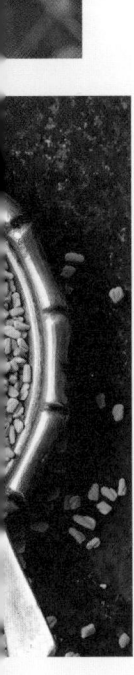

(Clockwise from top right)
Curry leaves; methi, or fenugreek seeds; and til, or sesame seeds, oil

Thalipeeth and loni, or white butter

Thalipeeth (*see pp60–61*) works well during this time. It is a quick, easy-to-prepare quintessential Maharashtrian staple. Many Marathi students take it with them when they travel abroad to study, as it serves as a versatile snack, breakfast, lunch, or even dinner. It's a fascinating dish because, unlike most Indian dishes that use a single type of millet or pulse, its flour, known as bhajani, combines a variety of millets and pulses with spices. Crafting the perfect bhajani is an art, and each family has its own secret recipe. To prepare it, simply mix bhajani with chopped onions and warm water, then cook it on a tawa with a generous amount of oil. The result is a thick, hearty meal that keeps you full for hours. Rich in fibre and amino acids, thalipeeth is a weekly staple in my household and we enjoy it with safed makkhan or fresh dahi.

> *"Thalipeeth . . . is a quick, easy-to-prepare quintessential Maharashtrian staple."*

A winter's afternoon

Lunch is at the centre of how healthy and happy you feel during the chilly months. Indian poets, such as Kalidasa, who flourished in the 5th century, wax eloquent of warm winter afternoons and biting cold mornings and nights. So, in India, winter lunches are planned as hydrating meals, to maintain proper electrolyte levels and hydration in the body. This is the time to celebrate kadhi pakoda (a dish made with dahi and gram flour) or turn the kulith (horse gram) into a kalan (a cooling drink) and contrast it with bajra bhakri (a type of flatbread). Amla (Indian gooseberry) is made into a murabba (marmalade) and winter vegetables into a sun-dried achar or pickle. And when you are hosting a lunch, you cannot miss sarson ka saag (a medley of nine different leaves), slow-cooked overnight and served piping hot with safed makkhan. The customary addition of jaggery and ghee at the end of lunch improves digestion, prevents constipation, and enhances the feeling of satiety.

Amla murabba

Winter produce

The beauty of bhakri

I particularly enjoy eating bhakri with pithla (see pp214–15). It is easy to digest and beneficial for those who have trouble with besan (gram flour) in other forms, such as kadhi, bhajia (deep-fried vegetable fritters coated in besan), or cheela (see p229). It also provides higher protein content compared to a watery dal. Pithla and bhakri is easy and quick to make and can be ready in less than 10 minutes. It can be adapted to serve last-minute guests in large quantities as well, by adjusting the consistency of the pithla. Additions of green garlic and onions to the pithla gives it a special winter touch and enhances its flavour.

While many may consider modak (see pp168–69) or puran poli the traditional delicacy of Maharashtra, the true staple is pithla with bhakri. There was a time when pithla–bhakri centres were set up across the state with the aim to provide nutritious meals in less than five rupees. The project, unfortunately, did not take off or else it would have been a good intervention to tackle malnutrition.

In Maharashtra, home to many saints such as Tukaram and Namdev, bhakri features prominently even in the spiritual traditions. In nearly all bhakti movements, each saint has composed at least one verse mentioning bhakri, highlighting its connection to spirituality and practicality.

In many communities, men learn to make bhakri because it is a simple and practical skill, especially useful for those who migrate for work. It tastes delicious even the next day, making it a favourite meal for farmers who often take bhakri with them to the fields for lunch. It tastes good even when it is not hot and is enjoyed when paired with raw onions and chutney.

This dish challenges traditional gender roles as well, especially in households where chapatis are often only made when the man sits down at the table, expecting them to be served piping hot. However, unlike a wheat chapati, which needs to be piping hot to be tasty or palatable, bhakri retains its flavour and quality hours after cooking,

Ragi, or finger millet, bhakri on an iron tawa

allowing for women to not be restricted to the kitchen and be part of the family meal. Unfortunately, the skill of making bhakri by hand is fading, as many people now rely on tools like the *chakla–belan* (rolling pin and board). I see this as a compromise.

Bhakri is thicker than regular chapati and it is unfortunate that, over time, its thickness has been undervalued due to the perception that the ideal chapati should be thin. Nevertheless, with its rich tradition and enduring practicality, bhakri remains a cherished dish that continues to nourish and unite people across generations.

The versatile rice

One of the most interesting aspects of India is not only the diversity of its cuisines, but also the diversity of its beliefs, of how foods are perceived differently across its many regions. Rice is one such food. In the north, a meal consisting of rice is considered hot, but cooling in the south. Therefore, while dahi chawal (rice mixed with dahi) is a cooling meal for lunch in the south, rajma rice is a dinner that keeps one warm during Delhi winters.

Rice engages with every aspect of life in India. Its harvesting takes place around Dussehra, a festival that celebrates Lord Rama's victory over Ravana and marks the coming of winter.

I fondly recall spending winter vacations as a child with my grandparents, at my ancestral farm in Sonave, a tribal village near Mumbai. One of my favourite pastimes was watching rice farmers use bulls to walk over the rice crop to separate the grain from the stalks. A few years ago, I realized that this method is not unique to Sonave. In parts of southern India, farmers place rice on the road and let elephants tread over it. While travelling to Naggar Castle, a 16th-century stone and wood castle in Himachal Pradesh, I observed a modern twist on this ancient practice – farmers lay out haystacks on the road and let cars do the threshing.

Winter specialities – green chilli, tomato, navalkol, or turnip, homemade mango pickle, green and red amaranth, and brinjal

A time of unique flavours

During winter, people often include specific ingredients, such as soonth (dried ginger), green garlic, and raw turmeric, to create distinctive flavour profiles. Soonth is an excellent way to add a hint of spice to dishes without causing stomach discomfort, mouth ulcers, or a burning sensation in the throat. Green garlic, another seasonal specialty, adds a distinctive pungency. Gujarati undhiyu (a mixed vegetable curry) is incomplete without it. Though green garlic has a short season, it is well-regarded for its heart-protective properties. This also illustrates that in Indian cuisine, nutrients are not isolated but incorporated as part of a variety of ingredients. While pickling is generally a summer activity, fresh pickles made from raw turmeric, carrot, and turnip are common in winter. Consumed within two to three days or up to a week, these pickles add an extra layer of heat to meals. Winter is also the season of kebabs, dahi bhalla (dahi-soaked lentil dumpling), and millet khichdi (millet-based one-pot meal).

WINTER

Spicy nightcaps

I am pretty certain that the tradition of nutmeg in milk as a nightcap originated during the cold winter months. After all, nutmeg aids in digestion, settles gas, and facilitates restful sleep. Cinnamon, nutmeg, clove, and pepper are the spices of winter, as is the good old turmeric. Drinking a glass of turmeric milk or masala milk, with a side of dry fruits, is another common practice during this time. All these keep the body warm and the senses calm. Spices are also used in almost all traditional winter sweets, combined with sugarcane in some form – liquid jaggery, hard jaggery, or brown sugar – and dry fruits or legumes such as peanuts for essential fats. A good example is panjiri (a dessert made from roasted whole wheat flour, ghee, nuts, and dry fruits), which is a common post-meal treat in northern India. Traditionally, a small portion of these sweets is supposed to be consumed daily, but this practice is declining due to misconceptions about the effects of sugar. Most winter sweets also require extensive dry roasting, typically done in an iron wok. Cooking in an iron vessel can enrich the food with iron, which helps boost our haemoglobin levels.

Haldi, or turmeric, milk

Tulsi, the sacred herb of resilience

Winters are also when tea morphs into both a pick-me-up and an immunity-boosting drink. Ginger and tulsi (holy basil) are brewed with the tea, boiled and reduced before serving. Consumed when one has a cold and cough, this tulsi tea has therapeutic properties. Tulsi, which not only grows wild but is also cultivated, is one of those foods that goes beyond nutrition to encompass deep cultural significance. One of India's most auspicious plants, it is considered a physical form of divinity and holds a prominent place in Indian culture. In Hindu mythology, Vishnu, the god of preservation, is believed to be in a deep slumber until winter. Upon waking, he marries Tulsi, the sylvan goddess, in one of his many avatars. The festival of Tulsi Vivah, celebrated after Diwali, marks the start of the wedding season and signals the opening of all auspicious wedding dates. This festival beautifully aligns with the seasons, as the tulsi plant nearly withers during the rains and rejuvenates and blooms just in time for the celebration. The tulsi variety that Vishnu marries is the one that believers bring into their homes, symbolizing the integration of the wild into domestic life.

> "... Tulsi Vivah ... beautifully aligns with the seasons, as the tulsi plant nearly withers during the rains and rejuvenates and blooms just in time for the celebration."

Besides being a popular addition to tea while it is brewing, tulsi is also added to some desserts such as kheer (rice pudding). However, it is not predominantly cooked, but eaten raw. Many households follow the practice of eating a tulsi leaf in the morning after bathing. This is not for any particular benefit, but a practice of faith. In fact, the tulsi leaf is also used in Hindu funerary rites; its leaf is placed inside the mouth of the dead. It is the last thing one consumes along with sacred water from River Ganga.

Imli, or tamarind (left)
Amla, or Indian gooseberry (right)

A homage to nature

In many ways, winter pays homage to the wild vegetables – amla, imli (tamarind), and ber (Indian jujube) – such that the uncultivated are tamed in the kitchen to bring out the best they have to offer. For instance, imli seeds are combined with buttermilk to make a refreshing drink; ber is offered to Saraswati, the goddess of learning; and amla is consumed raw or prepared as chyawanprash (a traditional Ayurvedic herbal jam), sherbet, murabba, or even achar. Some of these foods are also celebrated for their abilities to boost one's immunity. Amla stands out as it is a rich source of vitamin C, a nutrient that is typically found in high concentrations in amla. Its recipes are designed to ensure that vitamin C is preserved during preparation.

Every kitchen ritual celebrates the truly indigenous, conveying that just because something is wild or grows on the fence does not mean it is unwanted and should be trimmed. It is the wild and uncultivated growth on the perimeter that protects the planted and nurtured crops within the main farmland. Sometimes, it is the wild and uncultivated that protect the hearth and home.

Seasonal drink | Serves 2 | **Prep** 15 minutes | **Cook** 10 minutes

Amla–ginger sherbet

The original immunity-boosting drink with all the Vitamin C needed to support everything from healthy gums to a strong gut

In a bowl, add the grated amla and grated fresh ginger to 45ml (1½fl oz) of water and extract the juice. I prefer doing this manually, by squeezing the two, as that gives the best flavour and freshness. But, if you are short on time, a mixer followed by straining is also an option. Set this juice aside, and do not discard the dry amla–ginger pulp. We will use this for a second extraction.

Take this dry pulp and add 240ml (8fl oz) of water to it. Use a grinder to grind this and strain it using a sieve. This will yield a slightly watery extraction compared to the first batch.

Now, in a saucepan, pour in the thinner juice and stir in sugar. Boil until the sugar is fully dissolved, then add the thicker extraction and boil again to create a concentrate.

Once it cools, transfer the amla–ginger concentrate to a glass container. This can be stored in the fridge for a couple of days.

Whenever you feel thirsty, exhausted or tired, mix 1–2 teaspoons of this concentrate in a glass of water, add lemon juice and sendha namak, and stir well. Garnish with lemon slices before serving.

4–5 amla (Indian gooseberries), grated

2.5cm (1in) fresh ginger, peeled and grated

100g (3½oz) sugar

2 tbsp lemon juice

1 tsp sendha namak (rock salt)

lemon slices, for garnish

Something sweet | **Makes** 10 | **Prep** 30 minutes | **Cook** 20 minutes | **Special equipment** mortar and pestle

Til gul

Sesame with its natural oil and Vitamin E to add a dash of sweetness to all your relationships

In a shallow pan, roast til until the seeds begin to crackle, then transfer them to a bowl. In the same pan, roast peanuts until golden, then use a mortar and pestle to crush them into a coarse powder. Set aside in another bowl. Next, roast the grated dry coconut in the same pan until it turns a light pink. Transfer it to a bowl immediately to prevent burning from residual heat.

In a larger bowl, combine the roasted til, crushed peanuts, and roasted coconut. Add jaiphal powder, mix well, and set aside.

In the same pan, heat 1 tablespoon of ghee on medium heat for a few seconds and add jaggery. Allow the jaggery to melt and cook into a syrup. My mother taught me this trick – to test for readiness, drop a bit of the heated jaggery into a small bowl of water, then remove the droplet and drop it on a plate. If it makes a "tannn" or clang sound, the syrup is ready. Once done, turn off the heat and quickly stir the prepared mixture into the jaggery syrup. Mix well.

To roll the laddoos, grease your palms with ½ tablespoon of ghee, take small amounts of the mixture, and roll them into marble-sized balls. If the mixture cools and becomes difficult to roll, gently reheat it before shaping the laddoos again.

In Maharashtra, it is a cherished tradition to share these laddoos while saying, "*til gul ghya, goad-goad bola* (may this sweet add more sweetness to our relationship)". It is a beautiful reminder to spread joy and kindness with every bite.

150g (5¼oz) til (sesame seeds)

2 tbsp peanuts

30g (1oz) grated dry coconut

120g (4¼oz) jaggery

pinch of jaiphal (nutmeg) powder

1½ tbsp ghee, of which ½ tbsp is for greasing

Savoury bite | **Serves** 3 | **Prep** 20 minutes | **Cook** 40 minutes | **Special equipment** kadhai (optional)

Kothimbir wadi

The humble coriander typically used as seasoning gets to play the lead and impresses

In a grinder, grind the peeled ginger and garlic cloves along with the green chillies into a smooth paste. Set aside.

In a shallow pan, heat 2 tablespoons of oil on medium heat for a few seconds. Add til, the ginger–garlic–green chilli paste, and chopped kothimbir. Sauté until fragrant, then stir in haldi and salt. Add besan and rice flour, and mix well. Pour in enough water to soak the mixture and cook until it dries.

Take a plate and brush it with 1 tablespoon of oil. Pour the mixture onto it and tap it down while hot. Once it has cooled down and become firm, cut into square pieces.

Now, in a pan, heat the remaining oil on medium heat for a few minutes and gently fry the cut pieces. When the base turns golden, flip the pieces and fry the other side. Sometimes, for extra crunch, I deep fry them in a kadhai.

Enjoy these wadis hot.

2.5cm (1in) fresh ginger, peeled

2 garlic cloves, peeled

2 green chillies

250ml (9fl oz) oil, of which 2 tbsp is for tempering and 1 tbsp is for brushing

1 tbsp til (sesame seeds)

60g (2oz) kothimbir (fresh coriander), finely chopped

¼ tsp haldi (turmeric powder)

salt, to taste

120g (4¼oz) besan (gram flour)

30g (1oz) rice flour

Accompaniment | **Serves** 2 | **Prep** 15 minutes | **Cook** 4 minutes

Navalkol koshimbir

My aaji's signature dish, one that requires no cooking, only gentle handling

In a bowl, combine the navalkol cubes, crushed peanuts, and grated fresh coconut. Add the crushed green chilli and salt. Mix well to ensure the flavours meld together.

For an extra layer of flavour, heat oil in a pan on medium heat for few seconds and add rai. Once the seeds start to splutter, pour the tempering over the salad and mix gently.

Serve immediately.

1 navalkol (kohlrabi), cut into small cubes

50g (1¾oz) peanuts, crushed

45g (1½oz) grated fresh coconut

1 green chilli, crushed

salt, to taste

1 tbsp oil

1 tsp rai (mustard seeds)

Everyday meal | **Serves** 3 | **Prep** 10 minutes | **Cook** 30 minutes

Sheng amti

Shewaga may be a novel food for many but has been a routine in Marathi homes for ages

In a pot, place the shewaga pieces and potato slices and fill it with water, just enough to cover the vegetables. On medium heat, bring to the boil and cook until tender, allowing their flavours to meld together.

While the vegetables are cooking, heat oil in a pan on medium heat for a few seconds. Add the chopped onion and tomato, and sauté them until they soften and begin to release their juices. Next, add the minced green chillies, ginger–garlic paste, lal mirch, dhaniya, garam masala, and haldi. Sauté the mixture until it becomes fragrant and the spices are well-blended, creating a rich aroma.

Once the potatoes and shewaga are cooked, add the sautéed spice mixture to the pot. Then, stir in grated fresh coconut, powdered peanuts, and salt. Mix thoroughly to ensure the flavours are evenly distributed. Allow the dish to heat through, letting the ingredients come together harmoniously.

Serve hot with rice (*see p159*).

4 shewaga (drumsticks), cut lengthwise

2 potatoes, peeled and sliced

1 onion, peeled and chopped

1 tomato, chopped

2 green chillies, minced

1 tbsp ginger–garlic paste

1 tsp lal mirch (red chilli powder)

1 tsp dhaniya (coriander powder)

1 tsp garam masala

½ tsp haldi (turmeric powder)

50g (1¾oz) grated fresh coconut

50g (1¾oz) peanuts, powdered

salt, to taste

Sheng amti with steamed rice

Rice dish | **Serves** 2 | **Prep** 20 minutes | **Cook** 35 minutes

Vangi bhaat

There is no better way to enjoy a home-cooked meal than in the form of a comforting one-pot dish

Drain the rice and set aside.

In a pressure cooker, heat oil on medium heat for a few seconds, then add rai, curry leaves, and haldi, allowing the spices to sizzle and release their aromas. For an extra kick of heat, you can add sookhi lal mirch.

Next, incorporate the vangi pieces and fry them until they are well-coated with the spices. For added texture, I sometimes like to toss in vatane at this stage, mixing them in with vangi. Once the vegetables are cooked through, gently fold in the rice and add 250ml (8½fl oz) of water. You may have to adjust the quantity of water based on the type of rice you are using.

Stir in goda masala, lal mirch, and salt, ensuring everything is well combined.

Close the lid and bring to full pressure on medium heat, for 15–20 minutes. Keep an eye on the cooking time, as it may vary depending on the rice variety. Remove from heat and let the pressure release naturally before opening the cooker.

Enjoy it hot. I usually eat it with a generous dollop of ghee on top, which adds a rich, buttery finish.

60g (2oz) rice, soaked in water for 15 minutes

2 tbsp oil

2 tsp rai (mustard seeds)

sprig of curry leaves

1 tsp haldi (turmeric powder)

2–3 sookhi lal mirch (dried red chillies, whole), optional

2–3 small vangi (brinjals), sliced

2 tbsp vatane (dried green peas), optional

½ tsp goda masala (Maharashtrian spice mix)

1 tsp lal mirch (red chilli powder)

salt, to taste

Millet prep | **Serves** 2 | **Prep** 20 minutes | **Cook** 30 minutes

Bajra raab

Wholesome, comforting pearl millet drink to add warmth to the winters

In a pan, heat ghee on low heat for a few seconds. Add bajra flour and roast it, stirring continuously, until it becomes fragrant and turns a light brown. Stirring continuously is essential, as flours can easily burn if left unattended.

Meanwhile, boil the soaked jaggery with the water on low heat until it fully dissolves. Then, use a sieve to strain the syrup into the roasted bajra flour. Again, stir continuously to prevent lumps and achieve a smooth consistency.

To thicken, gradually pour in milk and stir well. Finally, flavour it with dry ginger and elaichi powders.

Enjoy the raab hot.

70g (2½oz) jaggery, soaked in 120ml (4fl oz) of water for 15 minutes

2 tsp ghee

30g (1oz) bajra flour

120ml (4fl oz) milk

½ tsp dry ginger powder

¼ tsp elaichi (cardamom) powder

Traditional taste | **Serves** 3 | **Prep** 7–10 days | **Cook** 2 hours 30 minutes | **Special equipment** kadhai, cast iron tawa, and wooden churner

Thalipeeth and loni

Comes with every family's own secret – this one is my mother's, best enjoyed with a generous dollop of white butter

To make the loni, every day, for a week, boil full-fat milk and skim the malai off the top of the milk, and store it in a ceramic or stainless steel vessel in the freezer. Continue this daily until the vessel is almost full. Once full, take the malai out of the freezer and leave it in a cool, dry place to thaw and reach room temperature.

In a pan, warm the malai until it reaches slightly above room temperature. This helps activate the culture more effectively. Remove from heat. Sometimes, I place the malai vessel on a hot tawa after making rotis, which brings it to the right warmth.

Now, add jaman to the warm malai and mix well. Let it sit in a cool, dry corner of your kitchen to set, usually overnight or for a few hours, depending on the weather.

Once the cream has set into a dahi-like consistency, transfer to a larger vessel. Add 250ml (8½fl oz) of water and churn the mixture using a wooden churner. The slow, to-and-fro motion of the churner is key – it retains moisture and preserves the delicate fatty acid bonds, which a mixer cannot do.

After churning, you will notice the butter has separated from the buttermilk. Wash the butter under running water a few times to remove any residual buttermilk. Do not discard the buttermilk as you can use it to make kadhi or drink it as is.

Loni is perfect when paired with thalipeeth.

To make the thalipeeth, we begin by preparing its special flour blend, known as bhajani. For bhajani, dry roast each ingredient separately in a kadhai until they split. Once done, grind them together into a fine flour mixture.

For loni

200g (7oz) malai (cream), skimmed from full-fat milk

50g (1¾oz) jaman (curd culture)

For bhajani (flour for thalipeeth)

1kg (2¼lb) rice

1kg (2¼lb) jowar

500g (1lb 2oz) whole urad dal (black gram)

250g (8¾oz) kala chana (black chickpeas)

150g (5¼oz) moong dal (green gram)

150g (5¼oz) ragi

100g (3½oz) dhaniya (coriander) seeds

50g (1¾oz) jeera (cumin seeds)

You can store this bhajani in an airtight container for up to 6 months.

For the thalipeeth, combine all the ingredients (except oil) in a bowl and mix well. Gradually add 80ml (2¾fl oz) of water and knead the mixture into a smooth dough.

Take a small handful of the dough and roll it into a ball between your palms. Then, gently flatten it on a sheet of butter paper with your fingers, shaping it into a rough, round disc. With your fingers, make 3–4 small holes in the disc so that it can absorb oil and cook fast. Repeat with the rest of the dough.

Now, heat a cast iron tawa on medium heat for a few seconds. Add a teaspoon of oil and spread it evenly across the surface. Let it heat up for a couple of seconds, then carefully lift the flattened dough from the butter paper and place it onto the tawa. Pour a few drops of oil into each hole.

Then, reduce the heat to low, cover the tawa with a lid, and cook the side in direct contact with heat. Once it turns brownish, flip the thalipeeth over and cook the other side, uncovered, until it turns brown as well. Once both sides are perfectly cooked, remove the thalipeeth from the tawa. Repeat with all the discs.

The unwritten rule is that the blob of loni should be atleast 4 times the size of a hole in the thalipeeth. Together, the two complement each other beautifully. There is also a scientific reason behind this pairing. Thalipeeth is made with millets, which can be difficult to digest on their own. In India, it is common to pair such foods with fat, as fat helps with digestion. Loni has fatty acids that aid in breaking down the millets and enhance digestion.

For thalipeeth

120g (4¼oz) bhajani

1 onion, peeled and chopped

¼ tsp haldi (turmeric powder)

½ tsp lal mirch (red chilli powder)

salt, to taste

2 tbsp oil, 1 tsp for each thalipeeth

*I love how winter brings out all
these unique flavours, such as
green lahasun and bajra.*

Green lahasun is a winter speciality that pairs perfectly with other seasonal ingredients, such as bajra and all winter vegetables. It is a key flavour in many winter dishes, such as undhiyu, the beloved Gujarati mixed vegetable.

But the combination that really stands out is the bajra and green lahasun laddoos. Unlike traditional sweet laddoos, these are savoury. They are perfect for days when you do not want to make a full meal. You can pair it with a simple dal, have it on its own with some chhaas, or enjoy it as a snack with tea.

This particular recipe comes from one of my team members, who is a Shia Ismaili, the followers of the Aga Khan. Every year, her grandmother makes these laddoos, and we all eagerly wait for them. It has become a tradition we look forward to – one that brings warmth and comfort in the heart of winter.

Seasonal special | Makes 5 | Prep 5 minutes | Cook 50 minutes, plus 1 hour of cooling |
Special equipment chakla–belan (rolling pin and board) and tawa

Bajra–green lahasun laddoo

A laddoo that you didn't expect with salt and spice

In a large bowl, mix bajra flour and oil until the flour is evenly moistened. Add salt, then gradually pour in 80ml (2¾fl oz) of hot water. Knead the mixture until you get a soft, pliable dough. You may need to adjust the amount of water to get the right consistency. Once the dough is ready, let it rest for 30 minutes.

Pinch off a small portion of the dough and roll it into a smooth ball between your palms. Using a chakla–belan, roll each ball into a disc. Since bajra flour is less elastic than wheat flour, it would not roll out very thin, so do not worry if the disc is a bit thick. In fact, this type of thick millet flatbread is called a rotla, which is very popular in the states of Rajasthan and Gujarat.

Next, heat a tawa on medium heat for a few seconds and place the rotla on it. Cook for a couple of minutes until the side facing the heat turns golden-brown. Flip and cook the other side until it turns golden-brown as well. Remove from the tawa and let it cool completely. It may take up to 1 hour for the rotla to cool down. If there is even little moisture, you will not be able to shape the laddoos properly. Repeat the process for the remaining dough – you should get 3–4 rotlas.

Crumble the cooled rotlas into small bits and set aside.

In a pan, heat ghee on medium heat for a few seconds. Once hot, add the chopped green lahasun and sauté until fragrant. Pour the sautéed lahasun over the crumbled bajra rotlas and mix well. Cover the bowl with a lid and let it sit for a few minutes so the rotla pieces absorbs the lahasun flavour.

Finally, take small portions of the mixture and roll them into medium-sized balls. Enjoy these laddoos as a snack on their own, or pair them with a dal for a wholesome meal.

120g (4¼oz) bajra flour

1½ tbsp peanut or sesame oil (filtered or cold-pressed)

salt, to taste

2 tbsp ghee

50g (1¾oz) green lahasun (green garlic), chopped

Unique prep | **Serves** 3 | **Prep** 25 minutes | **Cook** 25 minutes

Bhogichi bhaji

A medley of pulses and seasonal vegetables that takes your taste buds by storm

Drain the green toor dal, hara chana, and peanuts, then set them aside.

In a pan, heat oil on medium heat for a few seconds and add rai. Wait until the seeds begin to splutter. Next, add hing, curry leaves, and haldi. Stir briefly until fragrant.

Add all the cut vegetables and sauté them on low heat for a couple of minutes until they start to soften. Incorporate the drained green toor dal, hara chana, and peanuts. Season with salt and add 150ml (5fl oz) of water. Cover the pan with a lid and simmer until the vegetables are nearly cooked.

Meanwhile, prepare a paste of tilkut by mixing it with 1 tablespoon of water, then add this paste to the pan. Stir in lal mirch, goda masala, and jaggery. Allow the vegetables to cook completely until tender. Finally, add the grated fresh coconut.

Enjoy it hot with a millet bhakri.

30g (1oz) green toor dal (green pigeon split peas), soaked in water for 10 minutes

30g (1oz) hara chana (green chickpeas), soaked in water for 10 minutes

40g (1½oz) peanuts, soaked in water for 10 minutes

1½ tsp oil

½ tsp rai (mustard seeds)

¼ tsp hing (asafoetida)

sprig of curry leaves

¼ tsp haldi (turmeric powder)

1 potato, peeled and cut into cubes

1 tomato, cut into cubes

1 carrot, peeled and cut into cubes

1 brinjal, cut into cubes

4 shewaga (drumsticks), cut lengthwise into 2.5cm (1in) pieces

salt, to taste

1 tbsp tilkut (roasted sesame seeds), powdered

¼ tsp lal mirch (red chilli powder)

¼ tsp goda masala (Maharashtrian spice mix)

1 tbsp jaggery

30g (1oz) grated fresh coconut

Savoury bite | **Serves** 2 | **Prep** 5 minutes | **Cook** 30 minutes | **Special equipment** brass vessel

Chivda

The perfect Marathi snack for the road or the days when you crave a crunchy bite with your tea

In a brass vessel, roast poha for 5–10 minutes. Place the poha in the vessel before heating it to begin cooking. This prevents the poha from shrinking.

Next, in a pan, heat oil on medium heat for a few seconds and add rai, hing, curry leaves, green chillies, til, cashews, and sliced dry coconut in that order. Once the cashews and coconut flakes turn golden, add the roasted peanuts and chana dal, frying for an additional 5–7 minutes.

Then, incorporate haldi, salt, and sugar, mixing well. Add the roasted poha and churmura, and fry on low heat for 10 minutes, ensuring everything is evenly combined.

Allow the chivda to cool completely before storing it in an airtight container, where it will stay fresh for up to 2–3 weeks.

- 100g (3½oz) poha (flattened rice), sun-dried
- 2 tbsp oil
- ½ tsp rai (mustard seeds)
- ½ tsp hing (asafoetida)
- sprig of curry leaves
- 2 green chillies
- ½ tsp til (sesame seeds)
- 2 tbsp cashews
- 2 tbsp sliced dry coconut
- 50g (1¾ oz) peanuts, roasted
- 2 tbsp chana dal (split Bengal gram), roasted
- ¼ tsp haldi (turmeric powder)
- 2 tsp salt
- 1 tsp sugar
- 3 tbsp churmura (puffed rice)

Everyday meal | Serves 2 | Prep 15 minutes, plus overnight soaking | Cook 1 hour

Chhole

An all-time favourite across India, perfect with everything from puri to plain rice

Drain the soaked chhole and place them in a pressure cooker with 250ml (8½fl oz) of water. Bring to full pressure on medium heat, for 30 minutes. Remove from heat and allow the pressure to release naturally. Transfer the boiled chhole to a bowl and set aside.

In the same pressure cooker, heat oil and add tej patta. Allow it to sizzle for a few seconds, then add the chopped onion. Sauté until it turns soft and translucent. Next, stir in ginger–garlic paste and cook for a couple of minutes until fragrant. Add dhaniya and sauté well to enhance the flavours. Then, incorporate the chopped tomato, lal mirch, and salt, mixing everything together until the tomato pieces begin to soften and meld into a gravy.

Add the boiled chhole to the mixture, sautéing for a few minutes to combine the flavours. Pour in just enough water to cover the chhole, ensuring they are well immersed in the aromatic gravy. For an added depth of colour and flavour, wrap the tea powder in a muslin cloth, tie it tightly, and place it in the pressure cooker.

Close the lid and bring it to full pressure on medium heat, for 10–15 minutes. Remove from heat and after the pressure releases naturally, open the cooker and take out the tea bag. You can discard this. Let the mixture simmer on low heat for an additional 10 minutes, allowing the flavours to deepen.

Serve it hot with puris (*see p123*) and rice (*see p159*) for a delightful meal.

100g (3½oz) chhole (chickpeas), soaked overnight

2 tsp oil

1 tej patta (bay leaf)

½ onion, peeled and chopped

1 tsp ginger–garlic paste

1 tsp dhaniya (coriander powder)

½ tomato, chopped

1 tsp lal mirch (red chilli powder)

salt, to taste

½ tsp tea powder

SUMMER

The Sun is fierce, the Moon desirable… Nights with the darkness pierced by the Moon… and sandalwood are enjoyed by people… Travellers, their hearts burning with separation from their beloved, can't even look upon the earth, heated up by the fierce rays of the Sun, with its dust raised up by unbearable hot winds.

Kalidasa in *Ritusamhara* on summer, or गर्मी (garmi)

The season of simplicity

Summer is special because the scorching heat is not a hurdle but the very reason for flowers to bloom and mangoes to ripen. It is also the time for the harvest of cucumbers, gourds, and many pulses. In India, summer holidays traditionally meant coming together with extended family, mixing, mingling, and preparing food that would last. Making achar and papad (crisps) took precedence when it came to family activities, a practice that involved transforming summer produce into preserved items to enjoy throughout the year. This custom was about longevity and future-proofing our health. Achar and papad, though small additions to a meal, enhance every dish and reflect the way summer routines strengthened familial bonds and preserved traditions.

Today, many of these summer routines are fading. Air conditioning has replaced old-fashioned coolers, which cooled homes and added a pleasant fragrance. Long afternoon naps and airy white cotton clothes are becoming rarer as our traditional practices diminish. Winter food specialties such as panjiri (a dessert made from roasted whole wheat flour, ghee, nuts, and dry fruits), dal baati (a combination of lentils and baked wheat ball), and undhiyu (a mixed vegetable curry) may still be popular. However, summer traditions, such as rose, jasmine, and bael (wood apple) sherbets, are going out of practice. And even the joy around mango has been replaced by fear.

As climate change and heat waves become more prevalent, it is crucial to revisit the sustainable ways of handling summer from the past – methods that did not rely on electricity. One must remember how deeply summer traditions are connected to our cultural heritage and the need to preserve them in a changing world.

Mangoes soaked in water, before they are eaten

The king of fruits

Among the Mughal emperors who ruled India, Babur had a penchant for melons and never quite warmed up to mangoes. In contrast, Shah Jahan, his great-great-grandson, found that nothing could rival the sweetness of a mango. It is interesting to note that the emperors who embraced the mango often left a warmer impression on the Indian people than those who did not. The mango, it seems, has a way of winning hearts and leaving a lasting legacy.

It is sad to see, then, that mangoes – despite their rich diversity, with more than 1,000 varieties – are often misunderstood. Once celebrated as the quintessential fruit, mangoes now face a barrage of misinformation. Many believe that mangoes are detrimental for people with diabetes or that they are excessively high in calories. This is simply not the case. Fresh mangoes are a nutritious fruit that can be enjoyed in moderation by everyone, regardless of their health condition, without any ill effect on their health.

Incorporating mangoes into your diet is a simple and enjoyable way to enhance fibre intake. As people increasingly rely on packaged and processed foods, fibre is a key nutrient that often goes missing. Mangoes can help fill this gap. One mango a day can help ensure a regular and healthy digestive system. It is important to shift our understanding of food and adopt a balanced, commonsensical approach to nutrition, one that is not influenced by commercial interests, but grounded in holistic and sustainable dietary wisdom.

A versatile fruit

One can enjoy mangoes at every stage – from the time it is tangy and raw to when it becomes sweet and overripe. Each offering has its own unique flavour and use. Due to their abundance in summers, they are often substituted for other ingredients in recipes as well.

No part of the food goes waste. Raw mangoes are famously used to make achar and chutney, but they can be transformed into aam panna, as well. This traditional Indian summer favourite is a tangy drink, which is perfect for cooling off on hot days. They are incorporated into dishes such as ambe dal (*see pp218–19*) to create a delightful blend of textures and flavours. Even the seed is used in a few speciality preparations such as mukhwas (mouth freshener), to create a unique taste and flavour.

As mangoes ripen, they become juicy and firm, making them ideal for eating fresh as well as a great ingredient for aam ras (see pp122–23), milkshakes (see p100), and ice creams. Overripe mangoes are transformed into saath (a dried mango sweet with a chewy texture) or aam papad (dried mango fruit leather), which can be stored for months.

In India, there is often a friendly debate over which mango variety reigns supreme, with each region claiming theirs as the best. In Mumbai, the alphonso or hapus mango is revered to the point where, in the city, the term "mango" often refers exclusively to hapus. The period of mango consumption also differs across regions and communities. The Jain community, known for its strict adherence to nonviolence, refrains from eating mangoes once it rains to avoid harming the tiny life forms that may be present inside the fruit. The mango season usually ends in July, but the northern part of the country enjoys the fruit well into August or early September, thanks to the different mango varieties and tree types that thrive in that region.

The golden treasure of culture

Mangoes and its parts have a significant place in our culture as well. The leaves have antimicrobial and therapeutic properties. They are used to create *torans* (strings of flowers and leaves hung across doorways) during key festivals. The leaves also symbolize purity and auspiciousness and feature prominently in most religious rituals, decorations, and wedding ceremonies. Tradition holds that having a mango tree on the premises symbolizes prosperity and brings blessings to the home, making it an essential element in *Vastu*, the ancient Indian system of architecture.

Mango leaves also offer a unique reassurance. They signify that you are living in a place enriched with fresh food and promise cool shade. They embody optimism and hope. When used during prayers and rituals, they reflect a vision of a future filled with brightness and prosperity. During Gudi Padwa, a vibrant spring festival marking the start of the traditional new year for Marathi and Konkani Hindus, a special tradition involves preparing and savouring ambe dal. In the early evening, when women gather for Haldi-Kumkum, a ritual where women exchange blessings by applying turmeric and

SUMMER

Local and hyperlocal summer fruits

vermilion powder to each other, they indulge in ambe dal and sip on cooling aam panna, celebrating both the season and the community spirit.

Ambe dal, a quick and easy dish, reflects a thoughtful approach to preparing meals. The idea is to prepare wholesome dishes using seasonal ingredients, and without spending too much time in the kitchen. By choosing recipes that are not only cooling for those who eat them but also for those who prepare them, you make the cooking process more comfortable and efficient during the hot months.

Another classic mango dish that defines the summer season is aam ras. I come from a large family where my grandfather had seven brothers. Each year, we would gather for a special party centred around making aam ras. The mangoes were first soaked in a large bucket of water. Then, we would sit in circles and make aam ras, squeezing the fruit by hand, while ensuring that not a single drop of juice was wasted. The days we did this were filled with stories and laughter. An additional element of summers was if you had a *bagh* (orchard) replete with mango trees, you always sent an *aam peti* (mango box) to at least 10 households – a gesture rarely extended to other fruits.

The colourful berries

While mangoes may take pride of place in summer, this is also the perfect time to embrace diverse, hyperlocal berries found in every region across India. They come in vibrant hues, from yellows and oranges to delicate pinks and deep purples. Phalsa (Indian sherbet berry), jamun (Indian blackberry), shahtoot (mulberry), and rasbhari (cape gooseberry) – each berry has its own unique colour and flavour. For much of my life, many of these berries, especially shahtoot and jamun, were not market-bought, but picked and enjoyed straight from the trees. In smaller cities and towns, one can still see young children shaking the berry trees to make the fruit fall. Berries also symbolize love and devotion. In many regional films, young couples often meet under a shahtoot tree. In the Sanskrit epic *Ramayana*, Rama's devotee Shabari spends her entire life waiting for Rama, and when he finally arrives, offers him jamun. Berries might seem humble, but they are indeed fruits of great significance and symbolism.

Mangoes from the 120-year-old tree at Rujuta's ancestral farm

The creepers

The true mainstay of summer, however, is the array of creeper fruits and vegetables – lauki (bottle gourd), tinda (Indian round gourd), karela (bitter gourd), pumpkin, melons, and cucumbers – prized for their cooling properties. The *Hatha Yoga Pradipika*, a key yoga text, recommends incorporating cooked creeper vegetables into one's diet during summer.

Creepers, especially melons and cucumbers, also offer a profound lesson about life. These fruits start their growth attached to a vine, but as they mature, they detach and remain where they are – still connected to their origin, but independent in their new state. Though melons and cucumbers appear to grow together from a distance, they are actually separate up close, illustrating how one can live independently while remaining connected to the world.

The goal of human life is to grow in such a way that we can become detached from everything while retaining our sweetness. Just as melons and cucumbers may be bitter during their formative stages but develop sweetness when ripe, we too should embody a sense of sweetness upon maturity, despite the hardships we may have faced. This concept is reflected in the "Mahamrityunjaya Mantra", a verse from the *Rig Veda*, which is chanted to attain a state of life beyond death, symbolizing victory over mortality. In a way, the mantra honours the qualities embodied by melons and cucumbers.

A fortress with hidden nectar

A prime marker of this season is the coconut, summer's natural cooler, It is tough, rugged, and fibrous on the outside, yet reveals a sweet and tender interior . It reminds us that beneath a tough exterior, we can cultivate kindness and fluidity within ourselves. I love enjoying coconut water during the summer – its natural sweetness and hydrating qualities make it the perfect coolant. Avoid adding ingredients like chia seeds to coconut water as it changes its classic

(Clockwise from top left) kakdi, or cucumber; lauki/dudhi, or bottle gourd; and karela, or bitter gourd

Kopra, or dry coconut

taste. It is also best to look for coconut varieties available in your region, rather than the imports. There are different ways of eating fresh coconut as well. In coastal states such as Maharashtra, coconut sellers offer a range of options. They might ask if you prefer just the coconut water or a coconut with thin or thick malai (coconut cream). Just by tapping the coconut, they can tell you which type it is. If you prefer your coconut water to be optimally sweet, a coconut with thin malai is a great choice. These are the ones that are still developing, while those with thick malai are fully matured.

Coconut is so revered that it is often referred to as "Shreephal", meaning "God's fruit". The mature coconut, with water, is used as a part of prayer rituals. Once the water dries off completely, the flesh becomes a richer source of fat and is known as gola or copra. In the Himalayan regions, gola is used as a religious offering as it is valued for its longevity as it can last for a very long time without spoiling. This also makes it a handy snack for energy, especially for those trekking in the Himalayas.

Picking coconuts from the trees has always been challenging and while free-climbing the coconut trees has become less common due to the physical demands and a decline in the number of people with the necessary skills to do it, the fruit is thriving, thanks to new methods – from machines that help people climb coconut trees to shorter coconut tree varieties that are easier to harvest. It is these innovations and traditions that reflect the coconut's cultural importance and adaptability, and ensure its place in our food.

Endangered flavours

Although singhada (water chestnut) and kamal kakdi (lotus stem) are consumed towards winter, I want to use these to highlight a broader issue of preservation of less popular foods. To keep these uncultivated and wild plants thriving, we might need to understand our environment properly. These vegetables need small ponds with underground streams to grow, but with development and disappearing water bodies, their natural habitats are shrinking. Those who harvest them sell their catch right there, from the edge of the pond. They pull them out fresh, sell them, and then dive back in to collect more. This provides income for some of the most vulnerable groups in our country. Addressing the challenge of shrinking habitats is crucial for sustaining the environment as well as the livelihoods of those who depend on these valuable resources.

"... tamarind ... was not just a treat but also a source of nutrients that contributed to oral health."

Tamarind and kokum are two other remarkable foods that have unfortunately fallen out of favour, despite their numerous benefits. The Food and Agriculture Organization (FAO) of the United Nations classifies foods like them as "neglected and underutilized species".

In the past, tamarind was a common sight near schools, where vendors sold it as a popular, tangy snack. It was not just a treat but also a source of nutrients that contributed to oral health. It is a rare sight these days. The food's sourness, once cherished, is now less appreciated.

The tamarind seed was traditionally used in various ways, such as when mixed with chaas (buttermilk) for added health benefits, reflecting a diet rich in diverse nutrients.

Kokum, too, faces its own challenges. Climate change threatens the kokum trees in the Western Ghats of India, jeopardizing not only the fruit, but also the traditional uses and benefits. It is cherished as a spice, as sherbet, or eaten raw. It has fat-burning properties and is valued for its versatility. Kokum butter, known locally as kokum tel, is traditionally used to massage the feet at night, cooling the body and promoting restful sleep. Reviving interest in these underutilized foods would help restore their place in our diets and protect them for future generations.

Kokum and ranjhana

Fruit eaten right

When it comes to fruits, eating them whole is always preferable because that is how nature intended them to be consumed. It is wise to limit juice consumption to occasional treats rather than making it a regular part of your diet. It is best to enjoy one type of fruit at a time rather than mixing multiple varieties. For example, if you are eating jamun, just eat jamun rather than mixing it with various other fruits. Fruit chaat (mixed fruit salad) is an occasional treat served at weddings but should not be considered as a replacement for a regular meal.

A good time to eat fruits is either first thing in the morning, or as a mid-meal, or before and after your workout session. Generally, fruits should not be eaten along or immediately after your meals. But there are exceptions to this rule – banana, mango, and jackfruit. These fruits can be, and are, regularly eaten as a part of the main meal.

The power of pickle

Certain foods, such as achar, have an almost universal comforting appeal. On days when you are not in the mood to eat or cook, a simple meal of roti or rice with achar can be incredibly satisfying. Achars have long been a staple in Indian homes, serving as a natural source of beneficial bacteria long before terms such as probiotic and prebiotic became popular.

Pregnant women often experience a loss of appetite, but achar remains one of the few foods that can stimulate their appetite and ensure they get the nutrition they need. In India, there are two distinct types of achars made for different seasons. The pickles made in winter should be consumed within a few days, while those from summer can be enjoyed over a much longer period.

Every family has its own secret achar recipe. If there are a thousand varieties of mangoes, there are at least a thousand ways to turn them into achars. One of my clients once shared a fascinating family tradition. In her family, marriage prospects are evaluated based on the family's achar. They have two criteria – the family must make its own achar and it must be prepared in a way that preserves the fruit or vegetable's flavour and quality.

Another client told me about a unique tradition in her family involving a special achar made from amla (Indian gooseberry). This achar is reserved exclusively for women who are pregnant, and it has been passed down through five generations. It is consumed only during pregnancy and is not shared with anyone else.

Misconceptions about oils and fats often lead to people using lesser oil in their achar. This is unfortunate as the pickle then spoils quickly. There is also an inclination to refrigerate achar whereas pickle made in the traditional way was typically (and still is, in our home) stored at room temperature.

The magic of homemade dahi

While achar has been a beloved part of Indian cuisine, an essential component that pairs wonderfully with it is dahi (curd) and its derivatives. On a scorching summer day, a cool bowl of dahi or a glass of chhaas (buttermilk) is like a refreshing breeze for the soul.

But it is the home-set dahi that has all the benefits. In our country, it is often described as "*maa jaisa pyaar* (like a mother's love)", emphasizing that nothing compares to homemade dahi. Store-bought dahi often lacks the genuine taste and benefits of its homemade counterpart. Preparing dahi at home is simple and quick, and some families even make it several times a day. Just remember to use fresh milk rather than packaged milk. Contrary to common belief, homemade dahi is also suitable for eating at night. Similarly, to make chhaas from dahi you should hand churn rather than with mixers or electric churners. Hand churning ensures that the chemical bonds between fat molecules, vitamins, et cetera, stay intact, ensuring the taste is retained.

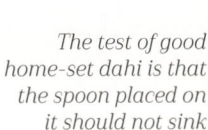

The test of good home-set dahi is that the spoon placed on it should not sink

The significance of homemade dahi is highlighted by a tradition in Gujarat, where a bride carries jaman (the culture for making dahi) from her *maayka* (maternal home) to her husband's house. She sets the dahi in her new home from this jaman to maintain the same beneficial bacterial "families" in her gut. This practice is rooted in the belief that gut bacteria are inherited. Introducing entirely new foods can alter your gut microbiome, potentially leading to discomfort or unease.

In the state of Punjab, during summer, there is a tradition of keeping a *matka* (clay pitcher) filled with lassi (curd-based drink) for everyone to share, helping them stay hydrated. It is usually the salty lassi, not the sweet variety, that is traditionally enjoyed to beat the heat.

Summer is also a wonderful time for making kadhi (spiced curd curry) because dahi naturally develops a pleasant tanginess. This sourness is perfect for creating flavourful kadhi or khandvi (a rolled savoury chickpea snack). The goodness of any food lies in its sync with the culture, climate, and cuisine, and must not be viewed from the narrow window of just nutrients.

A head start to the day

Summer days are long and hot, so a good practice is to start your mornings with fresh fruits or soaked almonds and raisins, as these are rich in fibre and have a cooling effect on the body.

Even though appetite tends to wane during the summer mornings, breakfast is crucial. Skipping it altogether can leave you feeling weak, sluggish, and prone to illness. While traditional options such as paratha or poha (flattened rice) are always reliable, consider incorporating summer-specific dishes such as amboli (see pp212–13) and ambli (ragi porridge). These choices are excellent for staying hydrated, maintaining electrolyte balance, and enjoying a light yet nourishing meal. They help you to stay energized and vibrant. Rethink how you end your breakfast. Instead of opting for the usual tea or coffee, consider a refreshing sherbet or chhaas. Office goers take tea or coffee breaks as a part of their routine to refresh or brainstorm ideas. However, offering sherbets in the office can be a great alternative. A well-hydrated workforce is likely to be more productive at work.

Summer provides a delightful range of sherbets made from ingredients such as kokum, lemon, khus (vetiver roots), variyali (fennel), and neem flowers, each with its unique benefits. For example, variyali sherbet (see pp98–99) not only aids digestion but also helps relieve foot aches, which are common during the hot months. Adding elaichi (cardamom) to sherbets and jeera (cumin) to chhaas enhances their cooling properties. Therefore, to beat the intense summer heat, it is essential to adapt our routines to stay cool and comfortable.

Variyali, or fennel seeds, sherbet

Summer rituals

It is always important to heed your body's signals. During summer, it is natural for the appetite to decrease. Eating less when you are not very hungry helps avoid unnecessary heat build-up. Overeating can lead to increased body temperature and sweating. By aligning your food intake with your natural appetite, you can maintain a balanced and comfortable state throughout the hotter months.

A key part of adapting to the seasonal requirements is embracing traditional practices. The use of neem stands out as a time-honoured tradition. Its leaves, fruits, and flowers are esteemed for their cleansing and immunity-boosting properties. In some regions, there is an annual custom of consuming the neem fruit, nimboli. It involves eating just a couple of nimboli, akin to receiving a natural booster shot. During Gudi Padwa, neem flower chutney is a traditional delicacy, consumed in modest amounts. Some people also add neem leaves to their bathing water to harness their antibacterial benefits. To further enhance your summer routine, you can add khus (vetiver) roots to your drinking and bathing water for a cooling effect. These practices are useful for preventing sun-induced skin reactions, such as *ghamoriya* or heat rash, which can cause discomfort and irritation.

Another versatile summer staple is pudina (mint). Historically, it was valued for its oral health benefits long before the advent of modern chewing gums and pocket mints. This herb can be seamlessly

incorporated into your summer routine – whether it is added to tea or sherbet, infused into drinking water, or blended into a chutney. Pudina chutney is particularly convenient as it remains fresh for nearly a week due to its lack of perishable ingredients, such as coconut or onion. You can also add pudina to bathing water for a refreshing and cooling effect.

Sabja seeds (sweet basil seeds) emerge as another excellent choice for the hot months. Known for their cooling properties, they become slightly pulpy when soaked and are often added to beverages such as sherbets or mixed into milk-based preparations.

An age-old technique for cooling drinking water involves wrapping an earthen pot with a damp cotton cloth. This technique uses the principle of heat exchange to cool the water inside the pot, even in sweltering temperatures.

Midday morsels and light fare

In the afternoons, as the heat intensifies, many people experience a significant drop in appetite. While eating less in response to your body's needs is appropriate, it is crucial to not skip meals entirely, even when you are too tired or nauseous to cook and eat. Skipping lunch can often lead to overeating at dinner. To prevent this, plan your lunches thoughtfully.

Incorporate foods that stimulate hunger and make eating more appealing. Traditional summer lunches are hydrating and easy to digest, avoiding heavy spices except ajwain (carom seeds) and jeera. Major spices are typically minimized to keep the meals light and refreshing.

A versatile summer option that is easy to make is rice bhakri, which tastes good even after setting it aside for a while after cooking. It is a popular choice during the hotter months and pairs well with simple accompaniments such as raita or paneer. Another refreshing summer lunch option is dahi poha (see pp101–03) for a light and cooling meal.

Roti with jaggery and ghee is another traditional lunch option. Jaggery may be considered a "heating" food but it has a different role in Maharashtra. For instance, when hiking in the Sahyadris, you might be offered a piece of jaggery before water. The belief is that eating jaggery helps cool down the system. It is also offered to young girls around puberty or those who have just started their menstrual cycle as it can help manage fluctuating haemoglobin levels during this time.

While the use of onion and garlic in cooking is reduced in summer, raw onions are commonly consumed because they help cool the body. In Maharashtra and southern India, white onions are often enjoyed as a koshimbir (salad) (see p104) with roti or with rice and dahi. Some even cook rice with white onions.

"In Maharashtra and southern India, white onions are often enjoyed as a koshimbir (salad) . . . with roti or with rice and dahi. Some even cook rice with white onions."

Rice plays a prominent role in summer meals. In Odisha, families often leave cooked rice overnight and eat it the next day for lunch. They mix the rice with dahi to make dahi chawal and typically pair it with something salty, such as pickle, papad, or sandgi mirch. A popular dish from the Konkan region, sangdi mirch is prepared by cutting the mirch (green chilli), layering it with buttermilk, and then drying it thoroughly. Once fully dried, it becomes non-perishable. Just before serving, it is deep-fried.

Red and white onions

Cool sips and bites

As evening approaches, many people turn to fruit because they are not particularly hungry for a heavier meal. This is a great time to enjoy seasonal treats such as mango or chikoo milkshakes as they provide a wholesome option. With increased consumption of dahi and chhaas during the summer, milk intake often decreases. A simple fruit milkshake helps ensure you still get the necessary amount of milk.

For savoury options, try steamed dishes such as khandvi and muthia (steamed vegetable dumplings). Lightly salted raw chanas (chickpeas) and peanuts are also excellent choices, as the salt helps stimulate your appetite and combat dehydration. A drink with sattu can also be a convenient and nourishing snack.

Winding down and sweet endings

The appetite makes an appearance around dinner, making it an ideal time to include legumes such as moong (green gram), matki, navrangi (a specialty pulse from Uttarakhand), and alsane (winged beans, a pulse from Goa) in meals. While pulses are enjoyed year-round, summer is a great opportunity to sprout them, before cooking, enhancing their nutritional benefits.

Lentils and pulses are rich in amino acids and fibre, giving them a unique distinction of being both a vegetable and a protein source. Unlike vegetables, which are high in fibre but low in amino acids, or proteins sources, which provide amino acids but lack fibre, legumes offer a balanced mix. If you prefer a simple preparation, consider turning beans into a refreshing chaat. Boil the beans and mix them with raw tomatoes, onions, and a touch of chaat masala (tangy, spiced seasoning blend). This not only helps restore your electrolyte balance but also makes for a satisfying and nutritious meal when paired with cooked rice.

After dinner, a variety of delightful sweets often conclude the meal. Shrikhand (see pp226–27) is a popular choice. For a fruity twist, amrakhand combines the classic shrikhand with ripe mango. Other favourites include kheer and halwa (types of pudding) such as banana halwa, which blends banana, coconut, and jaggery, and pineapple kheer, a tropical variation of the traditional semolina kheer.

To finish your day on a refreshing note, consider adding gulkand to your glass of milk at bedtime. This traditional Indian treat, made from rose petals and sugar, is prepared during summer when roses are in bloom. Beyond its cooling properties, gulkand aids digestive health by adding fibre to your diet, which can help prevent bloating and constipation. It also helps alleviate sleeplessness and is particularly beneficial for girls, as it supports healthy haemoglobin levels.

Seasonal drink | Serves 2 | Prep 5 minutes, plus 4–5 hours of soaking | Cook 15 minutes

Variyali sherbet

India's best-kept secret, a refreshing fennel seed drink that eases gas and bloating

Drain the soaked variyali and discard the water.

In a blender, place variyali, khadi shakkar, and add 60ml (2fl oz) of water. Blend the mixture until it forms a smooth paste. Alternatively, you can use a mortar and pestle to grind the mixture. Strain the paste through a fine-mesh sieve to extract the liquid concentrate. Discard the residue.

In a saucepan, combine sugar and 120ml (4fl oz) of water. Cook on medium heat, stirring continuously, until the sugar dissolves and the syrup reaches a one-string consistency. You can test this by lifting a small amount of syrup between your fingers to see if it forms a thin thread. In Hindi, it is popularly called "ek taar ki chashni". Be careful as the syrup will be hot.

Add the sugar syrup to the variyali concentrate and stir well to combine. Once it cools down, transfer to a glass bottle and store in the fridge.

To prepare the sherbet, take 1–2 tablespoons of the concentrate and dilute it in a glass of water. Stir until evenly mixed and serve immediately. For an extra refreshing touch, add some ice cubes.

2 tbsp variyali (fennel seeds), soaked in water for 4–5 hours

1 tbsp khadi shakkar (unrefined sugar)

60g (2oz) sugar

Something sweet | Serves 2 | Prep 5 minutes | Cook 5 minutes

Mango milkshake

A reminder that there is no such thing as mango lassi

In a blender, combine the mango pieces and milk. Sometimes, for an extra refreshing touch, I chill the mango in the fridge for 1–2 hours before blending.

Blend the mixture until it is smooth and creamy. If you prefer a slightly thinner consistency, simply add more milk.

Once blended, pour the shake into glasses and enjoy immediately.

1–2 ripe mangoes, peeled and cut into bite-sized pieces

375ml (12½fl oz) milk

Savoury bite | **Serves** 3 | **Prep** 10 minutes, plus 8–12 hours for setting | **Cook** 5 minutes

Dahi poha

A simple preparation of flattened rice mixed with curd, that doubles as a natural antacid

Let us set the dahi first. In a saucepan, heat milk on medium heat. Warm it until you can comfortably touch the vessel. Avoid boiling the milk. Once it is warm enough, remove it from the heat and pour it into a ceramic vessel. Add buttermilk and stir gently to combine.

Cover the vessel with a lid or a clean kitchen towel and place it in a cool, dry spot. Let it rest for 8–12 hours. The dahi would easily set within 8 hours in summer, but it could take up to 12 hours in winter. After the incubation period, gently stir the dahi to check the consistency – it should be firm enough to scoop.

Once dahi is ready, you can use it to make curd rice (*see pp105–07*), date raita (*see p111*), or masala chhaas. In this recipe, we will use it to prepare dahi poha.

Place poha in a bowl and add just enough water to cover it. Drain immediately. Then, add the dahi and salt, and mix everything well. Finally, garnish with a green chilli for an added kick.

For home-set dahi (curd)

500ml (17fl oz) full-fat milk

2 tbsp buttermilk

For dahi poha

2 tbsp poha (flattened rice)

2 tbsp home-set dahi

salt, to taste

green chilli, for garnish

Dahi poha with fresh green chilli

Accompaniment | Serves 2 | Prep 5 minutes | Cook 10 minutes

White onion koshimbir

A side salad of the rare and small onions to lend a sweet and pungent taste to your meal

Place the chopped white onions and green chillies in a bowl and mix. Add in the grated fresh coconut, peanut powder, lemon juice, and sugar. Season with salt. Stir everything well to combine the flavours.

For tempering, in a pan, heat oil on medium heat for a few seconds. Once the oil is hot, add rai and watch as the seeds begin to splutter. At this point, add hing.

Now, carefully pour the tempered mixture over the ingredients in the bowl. Give everything a good stir to ensure the mixture is evenly coated with the flavourful oil.

Enjoy it fresh with your meal.

2 white onions, peeled and chopped

1–2 green chillies, chopped

2 tbsp grated fresh coconut

2 tbsp peanuts, powdered

1 tsp lemon juice

½ tsp sugar

1½ tsp salt

2 tsp oil

½ tsp rai (mustard seeds)

½ tsp hing (asafoetida)

Everyday meal | Serves 2 | Prep 25 minutes | Cook 40 minutes

Curd rice and lemon pickle

Not your fair weather friend but a philosopher that appears on hot sultry days like a cool breeze

For the curd rice, combine the rice, 240ml (8fl oz) of water, and salt in a pressure cooker. The key is to use double the amount of water to rice. Bring the mixture to the boil on high heat, then reduce the heat to low, secure the lid, and bring to full pressure, for 12 minutes. Remove from heat and allow the pressure to release naturally before opening the cooker.

Meanwhile, in a small pan, heat oil for a few seconds. Add rai and once the seeds start to splutter, add the slit green chillies, curry leaves, and hing. Sauté briefly until aromatic.

In a bowl, whisk the dahi and then pour the tempered mixture into it. Mix well. Add the cooked rice and stir until everything is well combined. While you can enjoy curd rice on its own, I like to pair it with lemon pickle for an extra burst of flavour.

For the lemon pickle, in a blender, blend the lemon pieces until they form a smooth paste.

Then, in a pan, add sugar – the key is to use twice as much sugar as lemon paste. Pour in 250ml (8½fl oz) of water – it should be just enough to cover the sugar. Heat the mixture, stirring occasionally, until the sugar dissolves completely.

Now, add the lemon paste, stirring continuously. Add Kashmiri lal mirch for vibrant colour and sea salt. Continue to heat, stirring constantly, until the mixture thickens and you can see sugar crystals on the spatula.

Once cooled, transfer the pickle to an airtight container and store it in the fridge for up to a month.

For curd rice

120g (4¼oz) small-grain rice

pinch of salt

2 tsp oil

1 tsp rai (mustard seeds)

2 green chillies, slit lengthwise

4–5 curry leaves

¼ tsp hing (asafoetida)

125ml (4¼fl oz) home-set dahi (curd)

For lemon pickle

4–5 lemons, cut into small pieces and de-seeded

200g (7oz) sugar

2 tsp Kashmiri lal mirch (Kashmiri red chilli powder)

sea salt, to taste

Curd rice with lemon pickle

Isn't it fascinating how food traditions can travel and evolve?

Take dates and dahi. Their pairing, though not common in India, has a rich history. In traditional Arab communities, for instance, it is common to break the fast during Ramadan in summers with dates and dahi. This pairing is ancient and over time, variations have emerged.

Date raita and khichdi is one such example. With its subtle sweetness, date raita elevates the experience of eating khichdi by creating a delightful contrast. I learned its recipe from a Punjabi woman, whose roots trace back to the Sindh region of Pakistan. While I am not sure who taught her this, I know it is her family recipe, passed down through generations. Some people add roasted jeera to their date raita to enhance the flavour. But then they also add ajwain to their khichdi. It makes sense because the earthiness of jeera in the raita complements the sharpness of ajwain in the khichdi. It is this interplay of flavours that makes khichdi and date raita so comforting.

Rice dish | Serves 2 | Prep 30 minutes, plus 1–2 hours of soaking | Cook 30 minutes | Special equipment tawa, and mortar and pestle

Khichdi and date raita

My personal favourite, the dish I turn to when I am feeling low, to lift my spirits

First prepare the date raita, as the khichdi tastes best when eaten piping hot – if left to sit, it can become lumpy.

To make the raita, heat a tawa on medium heat for a few seconds. Add jeera and dry roast for a couple of minutes, stirring frequently to prevent burning. Jeera can quite quickly go from perfect to overdone, so keep a close eye on it. When the jeera is fragrant and lightly toasted, immediately transfer to a mortar. If you leave it on the tawa, it will continue to cook. Let it cool for a few seconds and then grind it into a fine powder with a pestle. You can also make extra and store for future use.

Next, in a bowl, whisk the dahi until it is smooth and creamy. Add the chopped dates, roasted jeera powder, and kala namak or sendha namak. Mix thoroughly.

To make the khichdi, heat ghee in a pressure cooker on medium heat for a few seconds. Add rai and as soon as the seeds start to pop, add hing, haldi, lal mirch, and goda masala. Sauté the spices until fragrant.

Next, add rice and moong dal to the cooker. Stir well to combine and allow them to lightly toast in the ghee and spices for a few minutes. Once the rice and dal are well coated with spices, pour in 200ml (6¾fl oz) of water and bring the mixture to boil. I like the khichdi to be fluffy, but if you like a watery consistency, you can add more water.

Secure the lid of the pressure cooker, reduce the heat to low, and bring to full pressure, for 20 minutes. Remove from heat and let the pressure naturally release before opening the cooker.

Enjoy the khichdi with a generous dollop of ghee on top and the date raita.

For date raita

1 tsp jeera (cumin seeds)

125g (4½oz) home-set dahi (curd)

3 dates, soaked in water for 1–2 hours and chopped

kala namak (black salt), or sendha namak (rock salt), to taste

For khichdi

1 tbsp ghee

½ tsp rai (mustard seeds)

¼ tsp hing (asafoetida)

¼ tsp haldi (turmeric powder)

¼ tsp lal mirch (red chilli powder)

¼ tsp goda masala (Maharashtrian spice mix)

60g (2oz) rice

30g (1oz) moong dal (split green gram)

Isn't it true that everything tastes better when it's mixed or ground by hand?

That is absolutely true. It is because using stone or wood to crush or pound ingredients preserves their essential nutrients, flavour, aroma, and colour, unlike a mixer, which can heat and degrade heat-sensitive micronutrients.

One dish that I always grind by hand is the dry peanut chutney. While we often think of achars and papads as the go-to non-perishables in Indian cuisine, Maharashtrian food offers a variety of such dishes, with dry peanut chutney being a standout.

But to truly unlock the full benefits of this chutney, I feel it is crucial that it is prepared the traditional way and paired with time-tested combinations. In a world of constant change, it reminds us that while many things may fade, homemade chutneys will always stand the test of time.

Millet prep | **Serves** 3 | **Prep** 60 minutes | **Cook** 55 minutes |
Special equipment mortar and pestle, and tawa

Lauki sabzi, jowar roti with ghee, and peanut chutney

Bottle gourd curry with sorghum chapati and a side of chutney – a complete, satisfying meal that takes very little time to prepare

Make the peanut chutney first, as it can be stored for a few days. Then make the lauki sabzi. Save the jowar roti for last as it tastes best when hot.

For the peanut chutney, heat oil in a pan on medium heat for a few seconds. Add peanuts and sauté them, stirring constantly, until they turn a light golden-brown. Be sure to keep stirring as peanuts can burn very quickly. Once roasted, remove from heat and transfer to a bowl to cool completely.

In a mortar, combine the roasted peanuts, peeled garlic cloves, jeera, Kashmiri lal mirch, and salt. Kashmiri lal mirch gives the chutney a vibrant colour without making it too spicy. Grind the mixture with the pestle. Since this is a dry chutney, it is important to use the mortar and pestle for the right texture – the ingredients should be pressed together, not just broken up as they would be in a mixer.

Once the mixture is ground, transfer it to a bowl. Sometimes, I eat this chutney with just a millet or rice bhakri (*see p215*) for lunch.

To make the lauki sabzi, in a pan, heat ghee on medium heat for a few seconds. Once the ghee is hot, add jeera and let the seeds splutter. Then, add hing and chopped green chillies. Sauté for a minute, until fragrant.

Next, add the chopped lauki and give a good stir so that the lauki pieces are well coated with ghee and spices. Cover the pan with a lid and cook until the lauki is tender, stirring occasionally to prevent sticking.

For peanut chutney

2 tsp oil

150g (5¼oz) peanuts

5–6 garlic cloves, peeled

½ tsp jeera (cumin seeds)

1 tsp Kashmiri lal mirch (Kashmiri red chilli powder)

salt, to taste

For lauki sabzi

1 tbsp ghee

1 tsp jeera (cumin seeds)

¼ tsp hing (asafoetida)

3 green chillies, chopped

½ lauki (bottle gourd), peeled and cut into square pieces

1 tbsp peanuts, powdered

1 tbsp grated fresh coconut

½ tsp sugar

salt, to taste

fresh coriander leaves, for garnish

Once the lauki is cooked, add the peanut powder, grated fresh coconut, sugar, and salt. Stir everything together until well combined. Garnish with fresh coriander leaves.

To make jowar roti, boil 120ml (4fl oz) of water in a saucepan. Once the water comes to the boil, add oil, stir it well, and remove the saucepan from the heat.

Add the jowar flour to the hot water, cover the saucepan with a lid, and allow it to cool. Once the mixture has cooled enough to handle, transfer it to a plate and knead it into a smooth, pliable dough.

Divide the dough into small balls by rolling them between your palms. On a clean, flat surface, sprinkle jowar flour and gently flatten each dough ball into thin circles using your hands. It is fine if they are not perfectly round.

Heat a tawa on medium heat. Once it is hot, place the rolled dough onto the tawa and lightly sprinkle water on the top side. Cook until the water has completely evaporated, then flip the roti and cook for another minute.

Next, remove the roti from the tawa and place the un-watered side directly on heat. Cook it until it is golden brown. Repeat this with all the rolled out rotis. Brush them with ghee for eating. You can enjoy this meal with a side of home-set dahi (curd) (see *p101*).

For jowar roti

1 tbsp oil

140g (5oz) jowar flour, of which 1 tbsp is for sprinkling

1 tbsp ghee

Lauki sabzi, jowar roti with ghee, and peanut chutney

Traditional taste | **Serves** 2 | **Prep** 30 minutes | **Cook** 15 minutes |
Special equipment cheesecloth/muslin cloth

Kokum saar

A must-have digestive that looks as good as it tastes

In a blender, combine the coconut pieces, green chilli, peeled garlic clove and ginger, sugar, and 350ml (12fl oz) of warm water and blend until smooth.

Next, take a sieve and line it with a cheesecloth/muslin cloth. Strain the blended mixture through it to extract fresh coconut milk. This is a flavoured version, but you can easily make plain coconut milk by following the same method with just coconut pieces, omitting the additional ingredients. Do not discard the dry pulp as we will use this for a second extraction.

Return the dry pulp to the blender, add 120ml (4fl oz) of warm water, and blend again. Strain this mixture. Combine the two extractions and add kokum agal.

Next, in a small pan, heat oil on medium heat for a few seconds. And add jeera and rai. Once the seeds begin to splutter, pour the tempered mixture into the coconut milk and kokum agal. Season with salt and stir well.

Garnish with fresh coriander leaves and serve immediately.

1 fresh coconut, de-husked and cut into cubes

1 green chilli

1 garlic clove, peeled

2.5cm (1in) fresh ginger, peeled

½ tsp sugar

2 tbsp kokum agal (kokum extract)

1 tbsp oil

¼ tsp jeera (cumin seeds)

¼ tsp rai (mustard seeds)

salt, to taste

fresh coriander leaves, for garnish

I wonder why we are reaching for supplements when we could be enjoying a mango instead.

Mangoes are not only delicious, but their low to medium glycemic index, and their rich profile of fibre, antioxidants, and phytonutrients makes them not just safe but recommended for people with diabetes and obesity. Yet, many of us still reach for green tea, oats or supplements for these same benefits. Why? Not because they are better, but because the food industry knows how to position, price, and package these products to attract consumers – a skill farmers, unfortunately, do not have.

So, this mango season, enjoy aam ras and puri at least once a week and make one day a "mango day" with the family. And remember, a mango a day keeps the fears at bay.

Seasonal special | Serves 3 | Prep 1 hour | Cook 20 minutes, plus 1 hour of resting |
Special equipment chakla–belan (rolling pin and board) and kadhai

Aam ras and puri

The perfect meal to celebrate mango, the king of fruits

For the aam ras, trim off the top part of the soaked mangoes where the stem is attached. Then, gently press the mangoes from all sides to soften them evenly. Once they are tender, extract the pulp by gently squeezing from the bottom upwards, allowing the juicy flesh to release. Set this aside while you make the puris.

For the puris, in a bowl, combine wheat flour, semolina, sugar, salt, and 2 teaspoons of oil. Mix well. Gradually add water, kneading into a firm, elastic dough. Cover with a cotton cloth and let it rest for 1 hour.

Once rested, pinch off small portions of dough and shape into smooth balls. Using a chakla–belan, roll each ball into a thin circle.

Heat the remaining oil in a kadhai on medium heat for a few minutes. If it is not hot enough, the puris will absorb excess oil and turn soggy. To test the oil, drop a tiny piece of the dough in – it should sizzle and rise to the surface immediately.

Carefully fry the puris in batches of 2–3, until they puff up and turn golden-brown on both sides. Drain and place on a plate.

Enjoy hot, crispy puris with a generous portion of aam ras.

For aam ras
2 ripe mangoes, soaked in water for 20–30 minutes

For puri
120g (4¼oz) wheat flour
1 tsp semolina
½ tsp sugar
1 tsp salt
500ml (17fl oz) oil, of which 2 tsp is for the dough

Unique prep | Serves 3 | Prep 15 minutes | Cook 30 minutes

Ole kaju usal

A tender cashew curry, a beloved delicacy of the Konkan and the western coast

In a pressure cooker, add ole kaju and bring to full pressure over medium heat, for 15 minutes. Remove and let the pressure release naturally before opening the cooker. Transfer the ole kaju to a bowl and set aside. Repeat the process for green peas (if using).

For tempering, in a pan, heat oil on medium heat for a few seconds. Add rai, hing, haldi, and lal mirch (if using). Sauté the spices until they release a fragrant aroma.

Next, pour in the fresh coconut milk (see p118), cover the pan with a lid, and let it simmer for about 10 minutes, stirring occasionally.

Incorporate the cooked ole kaju and green peas, along with 240ml (8fl oz) of water. Add salt and goda masala. If you like it extra spicy, you could add additional lal mirch. Finally, add jaggery, grated fresh coconut, and chopped fresh coriander.

Mix everything well and enjoy it hot with rice (see p159).

75g (2½oz) ole kaju (fresh cashews)

75g (2½oz) green peas, optional

1 tbsp oil

½ tsp rai (mustard seeds)

¼ tsp hing (asafoetida)

¼ tsp haldi (turmeric powder)

1 tsp lal mirch (red chilli powder), optional

120ml (4fl oz) fresh coconut milk

salt, to taste

½ tsp goda masala (Maharashtrian spice mix)

1 tbsp jaggery

½ tsp grated fresh coconut

sprig of fresh coriander, chopped

Something sweet | **Serves** 3 | **Prep** 10 minutes | **Cook** 15 minutes

Banana halwa

Only a creative genius could have made the sweet banana even sweeter

In a pan, heat ghee on medium heat for a few seconds. Add the chopped bananas and cook, stirring continuously, until the raw aroma dissipates and the mixture thickens.

Next, stir in the grated jaggery and grated fresh coconut. Cook until everything melts together and forms a cohesive mixture.

Add jaiphal powder and chopped nuts, and continue to cook for a couple more minutes until the halwa begins to pull away from the sides of the pan.

You can enjoy this delicious treat on its own or pair it with rotis for a delightful meal.

2 tbsp ghee

2 ripe bananas, peeled and cut into cubes

3 tbsp jaggery

40g (1½oz) grated fresh coconut

½ tsp jaiphal (nutmeg) powder

1 tbsp almonds, chopped

1 tbsp pistachios, chopped

1 tbsp cashews, chopped

Everyday meal | Serves 2 | Prep 15 minutes | Cook 35 minutes

Vaal usal

My grandfather's signature dish

In a pressure cooker, heat oil on medium heat for a few seconds, then add jeera and rai. Once the seeds begin to splutter, add curry leaves and chopped garlic (if using) and let the flavours infuse.

Add the chopped onion and sauté until it turns golden-brown. Then, add the chopped tomatoes and cook until they soften.

Add the cooked vaal and mix thoroughly, making sure it is evenly coated with the mixture. Season with the everyday Indian spices – lal mirch, haldi, and salt – and for additional texture, the grated fresh coconut. Combine well.

Now, close the lid of the cooker and bring to full pressure, for 15 minutes. Remove from heat and allow the pressure to release naturally, before opening the cooker.

Serve hot with rice (*see p159*) or roti.

120g (4¼oz) vaal (field beans), boiled

2 tbsp oil

1 tsp jeera (cumin seeds)

1 tsp rai (mustard seeds)

sprig of curry leaves

1 garlic clove, peeled and chopped, optional

1 onion, peeled and chopped

2 tomatoes, chopped

½ tsp lal mirch (red chilli powder)

½ tsp haldi (turmeric powder)

1 tsp salt

60g (2oz) grated fresh coconut

The Ragi Kheer Project in Sonave

In the heart of Maharashtra's Palghar district lies Sonave, a small tribal village, where my family's ancestral farm has stood for generations. Long before modern farming took over, ragi, or nagli as it is called here, was the lifeblood of the community. It was a part of every meal and its hardy nature meant it could thrive even in the toughest of conditions. But over time, as this millet got tagged the poor man's food, it lost its market and gradually got replaced in the fields by rice or other cash crops.

The general prevalence of poverty also led to high levels of malnourishment in the district. In 2016, I turned to ragi - a link to the past - as a possible solution. We started the Ragi Kheer Project as a simple intervention by serving this wholesome dish of ragi, milk, and jaggery to schoolgoing children for breakfast. Today, we reach out to more than 400 children and have seen huge improvement in all their development parameters.

Now, our hope is to reawaken the tradition of ragi farming, so that Sonave can once again go back to growing what was once its staple. It is a small step, but it feels like a big one, reconnecting our past with our present, and nurturing the future.

Millet prep | **Serves** 3 | **Prep** 10 minutes | **Cook** 30 minutes

Ragi kheer

Sweet pudding made with finger millet, milk, and jaggery – our breakfast project that helped with millet revival in the tribal village of Sonave

In a bowl, combine ragi flour with 180ml (6fl oz) of water. Mix until it forms a smooth slurry.

In a pan, heat 60ml (2fl oz) of water until warm, but not boiling. Gradually add the ragi slurry, stirring constantly. Once the mixture begins to thicken, add jaggery. Cook, stirring occasionally, until it thickens further and bubbles form.

Pour in milk, salt, and jaiphal powder (if using). Mix well to combine. If you are adding dry fruits, gently fold them in at this stage. Heat the mixture until it begins to simmer, then remove from heat.

Enjoy it hot for breakfast.

120g (4¼oz) ragi flour

130g (4½oz) jaggery

250ml (8½fl oz) milk

pinch of salt

pinch of jaiphal (nutmeg) powder, optional

50g (1¾oz) dry fruits, optional

RAINS

The clouds, bent with the weight of water, thinking "This is the raised shelter for us, who are weighed down by the water we carry," seem to be delighting the Vindhya mountain, which is heated with the rays of the extremely harsh summer heat.

Kalidasa in *Ritusamhara* on rains, or बारिश (baarish)

The season of sustainability

If there is one season that is deeply embedded into our country's cultural and social fabric, it is monsoon. Sanskrit poet Kalidasa's 5th-century lyrical love poem *Meghdoot* brings the season to life as it describes the country's landscape washed by the rains in all its dramatic glory. In Indian classical music, musicians use the raga Malahara to convey themes of love and yearning, often likening the monsoon rains to the tears or longing of a lover separated from their beloved. Hindi cinema plays its part as well, portraying the monsoon as a time of longing and love.

Within the romance lies the more practical side of the season, one of the reasons why it is always of particular significance in India. Agriculture plays a crucial role in the economy, and the timing and intensity of the rains directly affect crop yields. Accurate predictions of monsoon patterns are vital for planning agricultural activities, managing water resources, and ensuring food security. It is no wonder then that the season is a key factor in the country's economic health and market dynamics.

It is true, monsoon breaks the monotony of other seasons by offering a refreshing change, a way to stay practical and yet indulge in romance and emotions.

Foraging the wild and uncultivated

Monsoon also marks a shift in culinary traditions, introducing a variety of wild and uncultivated vegetables, marking an end to the wild berries and cultivated fruits of summer. This is the time for delicacies, such as patra or patrode (savoury rolls made from colocasia leaves), which connect people with the forest. Wild ingredients, such as lingdi (fiddlehead fern), make their way into our kitchens, enriching the culinary landscape with unique flavours and textures.

Rujuta with her mother, Rekha Diwekar

136　MITĀHĀRA

(Left) Monsoon special vegetables

(Right) Women sowing ragi, or finger millet, on the boundary of the rice field

Foraging for wild vegetables is deeply embedded in our connection with nature's bounty. Wild vegetables thrive in untreated, natural soil – free from pesticides and fertilizers. Mastering the skill of distinguishing between edible and poisonous plants is crucial for safe foraging. Tribal communities, particularly women, play a crucial role in this practice. They often accompany cattle into the forest for grazing or venture out on their own to gather forage. They are skilled in foraging wild and uncultivated vegetables, such as lingdi and colocasia leaves, which they bring back to prepare in their kitchens. Extreme views on cattle management can disrupt these traditional practices, where older women pass down their expertise in identifying edible forest foods to the next generation. For instance, identifying lingdi involves noting subtle details such as thread colour and stem size, reflecting the fine skills required for successful foraging.

Once gathered, these wild ingredients can be transformed into delicious dishes in the kitchen, celebrating the essence of "soil to soul" or "forest to table". This process underscores the deep connection between the land and our culinary traditions, highlighted during the monsoon season.

Sustainable practices

There are many other practices that reflect this theme of connection with nature. One could say that our ancestors demonstrated foresight even before the era of climate change. For instance, orthodox meat-eating families often forgo meat in monsoon due to concerns about the potential diet of cattle amidst vast and unpredictable wild growth. This is also why dairy products are less prevalent during this monsoon season. People avoid dairy in desserts as well. In my family, we opt for kesar bhaat or rice flavoured with saffron and spices and sweetened with jaggery, instead of the traditional milk-based rice pudding. Many fishing communities, such as the Kolis of Maharashtra, refrain from taking their boats out to sea during the monsoon – not just due to high

tides, but to allow fish to lay eggs, ensuring a better catch in the next season. This practice reflects their deep understanding of sustaining their long-term livelihoods.

On the vegetarian side, families may refrain from eating leafy vegetables because of increased risk of contamination from damp conditions. Even underground crops such as onions become difficult to access. Food practices are closely linked to crop cycle and environmental conditions. But, they are also linked to our cultural traditions and philosophical systems.

Sit, settle, and reflect

Monsoon offers a time to embrace a cleaner, renewed life. Just as the Earth undergoes a cleansing during this period, it's a reminder for you to start anew. It's an opportunity to abandon unhealthy habits and adopt cleaner, more mindful food practices. Use this time to let go of what no longer serves you, and begin afresh. Reflect, introspect, and realign your life's path. Take a moment to sit, settle, and contemplate during this season of renewal.

No wonder then that most monsoon festivals and cultural practices focus on cleansing. Hindus and Jains observe Chaturmasya, a holy four-month period dedicated to austerities and repentance. For Hindus, this is particularly emphasized during Shravan, the fifth month of the Hindu calendar, from late July to late August, when a strict vegetarian diet is followed. This time of dietary observances also aligns with spiritual reflection, as seen in the Jain festival of Paryushan. Celebrated in August or September, Paryushan involves a diet of millets and legumes, avoiding vegetables and greens, and concludes with seeking forgiveness from all those we may have unknowingly hurt.

In Maharashtra, rushinchi bhaji is a delicacy cooked during the Ganpati festival. As the name suggests, it is an ode to the simple way of life of the ancient sages. This dish uses all the native greens and is cooked without oil or ghee.

As the monsoon ends, cultural practices also shift. In Konkan, the festival of Gauri Ganpati marks the end of the season. During the *visarjan* (immersion ceremony), villagers prepare a communal meal with contributed ingredients, which is offered as *prasad* (offering). While Ganpati, the elephant god, is vegetarian, his mother Gauri prefers mutton and fish, indicating a shift in dietary practices with the changing season.

Cooking techniques

Paradoxically, the monsoon season is also celebrated for embracing deep frying. Many wild monsoon vegetables are cooked with minimal oil, which can reduce fat intake. At the same time, the light nature of meals featuring wild ingredients can leave one feeling hungry more often, making bhajia (fried vegetable fritters) with hot tea a popular monsoon tradition for snacks.

Steaming is also a prevalent cooking method. A notable example is patoli, a traditional Konkani coastal dish made by wrapping spiced rice flour paste and a coconut-jaggery mixture in turmeric leaves, which is then steamed.

(Clockwise from top right) Bamboo shoots; kantola, or spiny gourd; and monsoon food basket

Monsoon produce

This is also when one sees a variety of unique vegetables emerge. Bamboo shoots can be chopped and enjoyed as a delicacy. Shewla (dragon stalk yam) heralds the monsoon, appearing just before the rains and disappearing shortly after. Meat-eaters might pair it with mutton while vegetarians enjoy it as a curry with garlic. An interesting aspect of shewla is its consistent appearance in the same location each season, making it a key indicator for potential changes in the crop cycle.

Other seasonal vegetables include kantola (spiny gourd) and kurdu leaves (flamingo feathers), while ambadi (roselle) is used to make pickles, chutneys, or is paired with mutton. Mangoes continue to grow through the monsoons in northern India along with other fruits such as pears and apples, which are harvested in August and September.

Legumes become a dietary staple during this period because of the limited availability of regular vegetables. It helps that they are easily stored, do not spoil with moisture, and are rich in amino acids and fibre. Additionally, legumes are simple to cook and sprout readily in this season.

"Legumes become a dietary staple during this period because of the limited availability of regular vegetables."

In India, this is also the time for sowing and transplanting rice, which is an extremely labour-intensive process. Consequently, meals are kept simple, avoiding multiple dishes.

Pulses and legumes are now gaining popularity as green manure as they are natural fixers for nitrogen and good bacteria, making it amongst the healthiest options for soil health. Pulses, as mentioned earlier, are listed as both a source of protein as well as vegetable by the FAO,

as they have both fibre and amino acids, a rare combination in the same food or ingredient. As the world prepares for climate changes of the future, it looks to the past, more specifically our diverse pulses and legumes as a storehouse of nutrients for both people and the planet.

Keeping a balance

Start your day with dry fruits such as walnuts, cashews, or soaked almonds. For breakfast, stick to your usual routine. At lunch, maintain a balanced meal by including a variety of legumes and a wild vegetable at least once a week, and pair it with a pickle. My favourite monsoon lunch is steaming corn curry with rice or bhakri (a type of flatbread) and a side of achar.

For snacks, enjoy seasonal treats such as patra, patoli, bhajia, charcoal-roasted corn on the cob, corn patties, or peanuts boiled in their shells. In the evening, keep dinner simple and wholesome with options like khichdi (a one-pot meal with rice and pulses) especially after a heavier snack.

"As the world embraces climate changes in the future, it looks to the past, more specifically our diverse pulses and legumes, as a storehouse of nutrients for both people and the planet."

Alu, or colocasia leaves; shewla, or dragon stalk yam; ambadi, or roselle leaves; and laal math, or amaranth leaves

Lakshmi at the farm harvesting the colocasia leaves

Seasonal drink | Serves 2 | Prep 10 minutes | Cook 20 minutes

Rice pej

It is a drink, it is a meal, it is just rice pej. If I was smart, I would say it is the prebiotic infusion you need

Soak the rice in water for a few minutes. Drain and discard the water.

In a pressure cooker, bring 900ml (1½ pints) of water to the boil. Add the soaked rice along with hing and kala namak.

Close the lid and bring to full pressure over medium heat, for 20 minutes, or until the rice is tender. Adjust the cooking time based on the type of rice you are using. One of my colleagues uses ukde tandul (Goan rice) and adds kali mirch (black pepper powder) in the pressure cooker for an extra kick, but I enjoy my pej plain, as given in this recipe.

Remove from heat and let the pressure release naturally, then open the cooker and add ghee, stirring gently to combine.

Pour it in a glass or bowl and slurp.

40g (1½oz) rice (hand-pounded or single-polished or any variety available at home)

pinch of hing (asafoetida)

kala namak (black salt), to taste

2 tsp ghee

Something sweet | Makes 5 | Prep 10 minutes | Cook 20 minutes

Ragi laddoo

My mother's recipe that went viral, working wonders on skin and hair – proof that good things really do come in small packages

In a pan, heat 1 tablespoon of ghee on medium heat for a few seconds. Add ragi flour and roast, stirring constantly, until it turns golden-brown. Be careful not to burn the flour. Once roasted, transfer the ragi flour to a plate and spread it out to cool completely.

In the same pan, roast khajoor in 2 teaspoons of ghee until softened. Combine the softened khajoor with the roasted ragi flour, nuts, jaggery powder, and elaichi powder.

You can customize the flavour to your preference. I enjoy the taste and aroma of elaichi, while some of my friends prefer jaiphal for a unique twist. If you prefer your laddoos sweeter, just increase the amount of jaggery.

To shape the laddoos, lightly grease your hands with 1 teaspoon of ghee. Take a small portion of the mixture and roll it into a ball between your palms, applying gentle pressure. Repeat with the remaining mixture.

Garnish with slivered almonds before serving.

2 tbsp ghee, of which 2 tsp is for frying khajoor and 1 tsp is for greasing

120g (4¼oz) ragi flour

2 khajoor (dates)

2 tbsp nuts (almonds and cashews), powdered

60g (2oz) jaggery

¼ tsp elaichi (cardamom) powder, or ¼ tsp (jaiphal) (nutmeg) powder

3 almonds, slivered, for garnish

I sometimes feel sabudana wada is the perfect way to show some self-love.

I often hear women say that once they hit 40, they feel it is time to finally do something just for themselves. Do you know what I tell them? Make yourself some sabudana wada. If that is not an act of self-love, I do not know what is.

And while we are at it, let us bust a myth – sabudana is not just empty calories. When you combine it with spices, potatoes, curry leaves, and peanuts, and pair it with some chutney, you have got pure happiness on a plate. Crispy on the outside, soft on the inside – what's not to love?

Savoury bite | Serves 2 | Prep 30 minutes, plus 4–5 hours of soaking | Cook 30 minutes | Special equipment tawa, and mortar and pestle

Sabudana wada and chutney

Deep-fried fritters made with tapioca pearls, paired with fresh coconut-coriander chutney – Maharashtra's pride and joy

Make the chutney first, as the wadas taste best when piping hot. To prepare the chutney, heat a frying pan on medium heat for a few seconds. Add chana dal and dry roast it until it turns slightly golden-brown. Remove from heat and set aside to cool.

In a blender, combine the roasted chana dal, grated fresh coconut, chopped fresh coriander, peeled garlic clove and fresh ginger, green chilies, jeera, sugar, and salt. Add 5 tablespoons of water and blend until smooth. Set aside while you make the wadas.

For the sabudana wadas, drain the sabudana and then combine it with mashed potatoes, powdered peanuts, chopped green chillies, salt, and jeera. The mashed potatoes help bind the mixture, while the peanuts add crunch. Mix everything well until evenly combined.

Next, shape the wadas. First moisten your palms with a tablespoon of water to prevent the mixture from sticking. Take small portions of the mixture and shape them into balls between your palms. Then, gently flatten the balls into thick discs.

While you shape the wadas, heat oil in a kadhai on medium heat. It is important that the oil is hot – if it is cold, the wadas will turn out greasy. To test the oil, drop a tiny amount of the mixture in – it should sizzle and rise to the surface immediately.

Once the oil is hot enough, carefully drop the wadas in. Fry until golden-brown and crispy on both sides. Drain and put them on a plate.

Enjoy the hot wadas with the chutney.

For chutney

1 tbsp chana dal (split Bengal gram)

75g (2½oz) grated fresh coconut

30g (1oz) fresh coriander, chopped

1 garlic clove, peeled

2.5cm (1in) fresh ginger, peeled

3 green chillies

½ tsp jeera (cumin seeds)

¼ tsp sugar

salt, to taste

For sabudana wada

100g (3½oz) sabudana (tapioca pearls), soaked in ½ layer of water above it, for 4–5 hours

2 potatoes, boiled and mashed

2 tbsp peanuts, powdered

2 green chillies, finely chopped

salt, to taste

¼ tsp jeera (cumin seeds)

250ml (8½fl oz) oil

Accompaniment | **Makes** 300g (10½oz) | **Prep** 20 minutes | **Cook** 10 minutes | **Special equipment** iron pan

Curry leaves chutney

A delightful chutney for lunch, perfect for curbing afternoon slumps and post-meal sweet cravings

In an iron pan, heat 1 tablespoon of oil on medium heat for a few seconds. Add curry leaves and fry, ensuring they remain green and don't turn black. Remove from heat and let them cool completely.

In another pan, add the grated fresh coconut, til, and roasted chana dal. Dry roast these ingredients on low heat until fragrant, stirring frequently. Once done, transfer them to a plate to cool.

In the same pan, add another tablespoon of oil and fry the sookhi lal mirch until crisp. Remove from heat and let it cool as well.

In a blender, combine the fried curry leaves, roasted coconut–til–chana dal mixture, jeera, and salt. Blend until smooth, adding water to achieve your desired consistency.

This versatile chutney pairs perfectly with amboli (*see pp212–13*) or works even as a spread for sandwiches.

2 tbsp oil

20g (¾oz) curry leaves

60g (2oz) grated fresh coconut

75g (2½oz) til (sesame seeds)

75g (2½oz) chana dal (split Bengal gram), roasted

3–4 sookhi lal mirch (dried red chillies, whole)

½ tsp jeera (cumin seeds)

salt, to taste

Sweetcorn is so easy to find these days. Why not just use that instead of white corn in the kadhi?

Historically, corn came in many colours – yellow, orange, white, and even purple – and these varieties were the norm. Today, the sweeter version has largely replaced many of them, but its lack of distinct flavour and texture doesn't allow it to be a versatile ingredient.

White corn, on the other hand, has a neutral taste that allows it to absorb any flavour. I remember, when I was young, we used to roast it over coal. The taste was incredible, as it soaked up the earthy aroma of the fire.

In kadhi, white corn becomes an integral part of the dish instead of asserting its own identity. It just absorbs the tangy, spicy kadhi, so when you bite into the corn, it is like sipping the kadhi through it, like a straw. That's the asli mazza (true joy) of enjoying white corn in a kadhi. And unlike pakoris (gram flour fritters), which are often added to kadhi, using white corn requires no extra work.

Everyday meal | Serves 2 | Prep 15 minutes | Cook 40 minutes

White corn in kadhi and rice

Move over Asian curries, the Bhartiya naari, sorry kadhi, is here

In a grinder, add grated fresh coconut, kali mirch, and ½ teaspoon of jeera. Grind together to form a dry mixture. Add 180ml (6fl oz) of water and grind again. Now, strain the mixture through a fine sieve to extract the coconut milk. Set aside and discard the residue.

In a pan, heat ghee on medium heat for a few seconds, then add remaining jeera and allow the seeds to sizzle and release their aroma. Add the chopped pieces of white corn, shewaga, and yam to the pan. Sauté these vegetables for a couple of minutes and then add the peanuts. Sauté for another minute so that peanuts are lightly roasted in the ghee.

Pour in 250ml (8½fl oz) of water and season with salt. Stir everything together and cover the pan. Let the mixture cook on medium heat until the vegetables become tender. You can check the vegetables for doneness by gently pressing them. You should be able to press into the vegetables.

Once the vegetables are cooked through, remove the pan from heat. Add the coconut milk into the mixture. This is a crucial step – be sure to remove the pan from heat before adding the coconut milk, otherwise it could curdle. Give everything a good stir.

This may not be the classic Indian kadhi that uses besan (gram flour) but still pairs really well with rice.

To make rice, in a pressure cooker, add the rinsed rice and 450ml (15¼fl oz) of water. The key is to use twice as much water as rice. Then, bring the mixture to the boil on high heat. Once it starts bubbling, reduce the heat to low. Secure the lid and bring to full pressure, for 15 minutes. Remove from heat and allow the pressure to release naturally before opening the cooker.

Enjoy white corn in kadhi and rice hot.

½ fresh coconut, grated

3 kali mirch (black peppercorns)

1 tsp jeera (cumin seeds), of which ½ tsp is for flavouring the coconut milk

1 tbsp ghee

½ white corn, cut horizontally

½ shewaga (drumstick), cut horizontally

50g (1¾oz) yam, cut into small pieces

40g (1½oz) peanuts

salt, to taste

120g (4¼oz) rice, rinsed

Who would have thought the humble yam could be such a powerhouse, right?

Historically cultivated in Asia, Africa, and Latin America, yam is a nutrient-packed vegetable, but often overshadowed by the likes of asparagus and broccoli. It offers loads of health benefits, from helping with bloating, constipation, and acidity to rejuvenating ageing skin.

You can turn it into a tasty sabzi or fry it into crispy kaap (fritters), perfect with rice dishes like masala bhaat. Yam kaap makes a great after-school snack for kids or a wholesome treat for elderly family members recovering from illness. Yam is also India's original mock meat, used by meat-eating families on days they abstain from meat, as well as a popular fasting food. Pretty versatile for such a humble veggie, right?

Rice dish | Serves 2 | Prep 1 hour | Cook 55 minutes | Special equipment cast iron tawa

Masala bhaat and yam kaap

Rice, spiced just right, with yam, the original mock meat, to capture everything beautiful about the rains

For the masala bhaat, heat oil in a pan on medium heat for a few seconds. Add rai and once the seeds start to splutter, add hing, lal mirch, and haldi. Next, drain the soaked rice and discard the water. Now, add the drained rice, peas, and cashews. Stir together until the rice gets a glossy coating.

In a separate pan, bring 450ml (15¼fl oz) of water to the boil. Once it is boiling, pour it over the rice mixture along with salt, dhana jiru, and goda masala. Cook on medium heat until the water is absorbed. Stir in the home-set dahi and ghee, then cover the pan with a lid. Reduce the heat and let the rice cook for 10–15 minutes. If your cooktop does not have a low heat setting, place a tawa on direct heat and set the pan on top to control the heat.

Here is a quick trick to check if the masala bhaat is ready. Sprinkle a little water on the kitchen counter. Without lifting the lid, place the pan of rice on the wet surface. If it sizzles, it is done.

For the yam kaap, cut the yam into slices, preferably ½cm (¼in) in thickness. Peel the slices and then cut them into thin strips. Cut each strip into 4 equal pieces – ensuring they are roughly uniform in size for even cooking. In a pressure cooker, add 250ml (8½fl oz) of water, kokum water, the yam pieces, and a pinch of salt. Secure the lid and bring the cooker to full pressure on medium heat, for 7–10 minutes. Remove from heat and allow the pressure to release naturally before opening the cooker. Carefully remove the yam pieces and discard the water. Let the yam cool completely. Meanwhile, prepare the coating mixture. In a bowl, combine rice flour, semolina, lal mirch, salt, hing, and haldi. Once the yam pieces have cooled, gently toss them in the flour mixture to evenly coated all sides.

Next, in a cast iron tawa, heat oil on medium heat for a few seconds. Carefully place the coated yam pieces on the tawa. Fry the pieces on each side, turning them carefully until both sides are golden-brown and crispy. Once fried, drain and place the fried pieces on a plate. Finally, garnish the masala bhaat with fresh coriander leaves and grated fresh coconut, and enjoy it with crispy yam kaap and dahi.

For masala bhaat

3 tsp oil

½ tsp rai (mustard seeds)

¼ tsp hing (asafoetida)

½ tsp lal mirch (red chilli powder)

½ tsp haldi (turmeric powder)

120g (4¼oz) rice, soaked in water for 30 minutes

75g (2½oz) peas

75g (2½oz) cashews

salt, to taste

1 tsp dhana jiru (spice mix of coriander and cumin seeds)

½ tsp goda masala (Maharashtrian spice mix)

1 tsp home-set dahi (curd)

2 tsp ghee

fresh coriander leaves, for garnish

grated fresh coconut, for garnish

For yam kaap

100ml (3½fl oz) kokum water (soak 1–2 dried kokum pieces in 100ml (3½fl oz) of water for 30 minutes, then drain)

180g (6¼oz) yam

1 tbsp rice flour

1 tbsp semolina

½ tsp lal mirch (red chilli powder)

salt, to taste

⅓ tsp hing (asafoetida)

½ tsp haldi (turmeric powder)

1 tbsp oil

Peanuts are my favourite tea-time snack.

Peanut is a versatile, nutrient-dense food that packs a punch with protein, healthy fats, and essential vitamins. It is a powerhouse for a healthy heart and glowing skin.

A popular myth is that peanuts are fattening, when in fact, it is a powerhouse of nutrients such as amino acids, essential fats, and vitamins. Whether roasted, added to a bhaji or koshimbir for a satisfying crunch, or blended into a non-perishable chutney, peanuts elevate any dish with their delightful texture and taste.

Millet prep | **Serves** 2 | **Prep** 30 minutes | **Cook** 40 minutes

Danyachi amti and vari tandul

Don't judge a book by its cover, or barnyard millet by its looks – both are full of surprises waiting to be discovered

To make the danyachi amti, drain the kokum and set aside.

In a pan, dry roast peanuts on medium heat until it turns slightly brown. Let it cool completely and then remove the skins. This step can take a few minutes, but it is essential for getting the right texture. In a blender, combine the roasted peanuts, green chilli, salt, and 4 tablespoons of water. Blend everything into a smooth, fine paste. In a saucepan, mix the peanut paste with 375ml (12½fl oz) of water. Place it on medium heat and bring the mixture to boil. Once it starts boiling, lower the heat and let it simmer, stirring occasionally, until it thickens.

Stir in the kokum and jaggery. The kokum adds a nice tangy flavour, while the jaggery gives it a subtle sweetness. Let it simmer for a couple more minutes so the flavours meld together.

In a small pan, heat ghee on medium heat for a few seconds. Add jeera and once the seeds start to splutter, add hing and curry leaves. Sauté for a minute or two until the spices become fragrant and the curry leaves turn crisp.

Pour this tempered mixture into the saucepan with the peanut gravy and give it a good stir. Let everything cook for another minute or so and then remove from heat.

As this curry is usually eaten during religious fasts, you can pair it with vari tandul, the fasting rice. Vari tandul is called "rice", but it is actually a millet and not a grain. It is made exactly like regular rice, just the quantity of water required to cook this is slightly more than regular rice.

To make this dish, in a pressure cooker, add the rinsed vari tandul and 600ml (1 pint) of water. Secure the lid and bring to full pressure on medium heat, for 20 minutes. Remove from heat and let the pressure release naturally before opening the lid.

Fluff the rice gently with a fork and enjoy it with the danyachi amti.

2 dried kokum, soaked for 20 minutes

75g (2½oz) peanuts

1 green chilli

salt, to taste

1 tbsp jaggery

½ tbsp ghee

½ tsp jeera (cumin seeds)

¼ tsp hing (asafoetida)

3–4 curry leaves

120g (4¼oz) vari tandul (barnyard millet), rinsed

Traditional taste | **Makes** 4 | **Prep** 30 minutes | **Cook** 20 minutes |
Special equipment steaming plate or steamer, and chakla–belan (rolling pin and board)

Ukadiche modak

The sweetest way to overcome any obstacle, and a must-have offering on the festival of Ganesha Chaturthi

To prepare the ukad, boil 4 tablespoons of water in a pan. Once the water starts to boil, season it with ¼ tablespoon of ghee and salt. Next, gradually add rice flour, stirring well to combine. Then, cover the pan with a lid and steam the mixture on low heat for 5 minutes. Once done, set it aside to cool.

To make the puran, take another pan and heat on medium heat. Add the grated fresh coconut and sauté until it turns golden-brown. Then, add the grated jaggery, stirring constantly until the jaggery melts and the mixture thickens. Remove from heat and stir in elaichi and jaiphal powders. Allow the stuffing to cool slightly.

Now my favourite part – assembling the modaks. Pinch off small balls of the dough and using chakla–belan, roll them into thin circles. Place a spoonful of the puran in the centre of each rolled-out dough circle. Now, grease your palms with ½ tablespoon of ghee to prevent sticking. Gather the edges of the circle to form pleats, pinching them together at the top to seal the modak into a pleated dumpling shape.

Next, it is time to steam the modaks. For this, take a steaming plate and brush its base with the remaining ghee to prevent sticking. Arrange the modaks on it in a way that they do not touch each other. Place the plate in a pressure cooker or a steamer and steam for 15–20 minutes over medium heat. Some pressure cookers may require you to remove the whistle.

Once the modaks are steamed, garnish them with kesar for a colourful touch. Enjoy them with family and friends.

For the ukad (dough)

1¼ tbsp ghee, of which ¼ tbsp is for seasoning, ½ tbsp is for greasing, and ½ tbsp is for brushing

pinch of salt

60g (2oz) rice flour

For the puran (stuffing)

2 tsp ghee

40g (1½oz) grated fresh coconut

40g (1½oz) jaggery, grated

¼ tsp elaichi (cardamom) powder

¼ tsp jaiphal (nutmeg) powder

kesar (saffron strands), soaked in warm milk for 30 minutes, for garnish

Seasonal special | Serves 3 | Prep 10 minutes | Cook 30 minutes

Narali bhaat

Traditionally made on Narali Purnima, celebrated to mark the beginning of the fishing season, when coconut is offered to the god of the sea

Drain the soaked rice and set aside. Discard the water.

In a pressure cooker, heat ghee for a few seconds and add cashews and almonds. For a fragrant touch, you could also add laung. Let them sizzle, then add the soaked rice and fry everything together.

When the rice is halfway cooked, fold in the grated fresh coconut and continue frying until the mixture turns golden-brown.

Meanwhile, in a separate pan, combine water and jaggery and bring the mixture to the boil. Once it starts to boil, pour this jaggery syrup over the rice mixture and stir well to blend the flavours. Sprinkle in jaiphal or elaichi powder to enhance the aroma.

Secure the lid and bring the pressure cooker to full pressure on medium heat, for 15 minutes. Let the pressure release naturally before opening.

You could garnish with chopped nuts and a generous dollop of ghee before serving.

2 tsp ghee

5 cashews

5 almonds

1–2 laung (cloves), optional

100g (3½oz) rice, soaked in water for 10 minutes

60g (2oz) grated fresh coconut

150g (5¼oz) jaggery

½ tsp jaiphal (nutmeg) powder, or elaichi (cardamom) powder

Isn't it amazing how something as simple as shewla can bring such variety to our meals?

Shewla is a wild and uncultivated vegetable that is packed with fibre, minerals, vitamins, and antioxidants. What makes it truly special, however, is how versatile it is – it can be enjoyed by almost everyone. Vegetarians pair it with garlic, fish eaters with prawns, and meat lovers with mutton.

These uncultivated vegetables typically grow in specific regions and are available only for a short time. It is because of their seasonal nature that they add diversity to our thalis. Unfortunately, as we drift away from these traditional foods, we miss out on their nutritional benefits and the skills needed to incorporate them into our daily diets.

For me, eating these wild vegetables is a way to honour my roots. Whenever I visit my ancestral home in Sonave during the rains, I make it a point to search for shewla in the backyard and enjoy its bhaji with puris.

Unique prep | **Serves** 2 | **Prep** 30 minutes | **Cook** 30 minutes

Shewla bhaji

As wild as it gets – a limited edition curry made with dragon stalk yam

First prepare the vegetables. For the shewla, cut the stalk and discard it as it is tough and inedible. Chop the rest horizontally into small pieces. Cut the kakda into horizontal slices and remove the seeds. Grind the kakda pieces into a smooth paste in a blender.

In a pressure cooker, heat oil on medium heat for a few seconds. Once the oil is hot, add rai and let the seeds splutter. Then, add hing and haldi. Sauté for a minute until fragrant. Add the chopped onions and minced garlic cloves to the cooker. Sauté until the onions turn translucent and soften.

Add the chopped shewla and the kakda paste. Stir well to combine. Season the mixture with lal mirch, salt, grated fresh coconut, and garam masala for added depth of flavour. Stir everything together and let the spices coat the vegetables.

Secure the lid of the pressure cooker and bring it to full pressure on medium heat, for 15 minutes. Remove from heat and let the pressure release naturally before opening the cooker.

Pair it with hot, fluffy puris (*see p123*), bhakri, or rice (*see p159*) for a satisfying meal.

½ bunch shewla (dragon stalk yam)

3 kakda

4 tsp oil

½ tsp rai (mustard seeds)

⅓ tsp hing (asafoetida)

½ tsp haldi (turmeric powder)

2 onions, finely chopped

4 garlic cloves, peeled and minced

½ tsp lal mirch (red chilli powder)

salt, to taste

1 tbsp grated fresh coconut

1 tsp garam masala

If we embraced foods like alu that tie us to farm and forest, wouldn't we appreciate the farmers who grow them so much more?

Alu or arbi (colocasia) has a pan-India appeal, but the wild vegetable has a special place in the hearts of Maharashtrians during the rains. It is during this time that we transform it into the beloved alu wadi, a festive must-have.

What is interesting is that alu is actually uncultivated. I remember a child once referring to it as an "automatic plant", which made me reflect on how we tend to overcomplicate food. It is a bit sad, really, that these wild and uncultivated vegetables, along with the traditional skills of foraging them, are gradually disappearing. We often forget that true nourishment comes from simplicity — rooted in farms, forests, and family traditions passed down through generations.

If we could embrace this mindset, we would begin to see alu differently — not just as an ingredient, but as part of a larger story about sustainability and tradition.

Savoury bite | **Serves** 2 | **Prep** 40 minutes | **Cook** 40 minutes | **Special equipment** steamer and kadhai

Alu wadi

The wild leaf, transformed into a dish that is perfect on its own or as a side, is a favourite across all regions of India

Cut the stalk and flatten the leaf, to make rolling easier. Set the leaves aside.

In a large bowl, combine besan, rice flour, salt, haldi, lal mirch, dhaniya, jeera powder, tamarind extract, and jaggery. Gradually add 120ml (4fl oz) of water and mix to form a smooth paste. The consistency should be thick enough to spread over the leaves easily with your hands.

Take the first leaf and evenly spread the paste on its underside. Take the second leaf and apply the paste on its underside as well. Repeat with the remaining leaves. Once all the leaves are coated, carefully stack them on top of one another. Then, roll the stacked leaves tightly – the paste will hold them together as you go. Next, place the rolled stack on the perforated plate of a steamer. Steam it for 10–15 minutes on medium heat, until the leaves soften. You will notice that the roll has lost its vibrant green colour. If you do not have a steamer, you can cook it in a pressure cooker on medium heat, for 7–10 minutes, for the same result. Remove and allow it to cool completely. Slice the roll horizontally into even pieces. You can adjust the thickness to your preference.

Heat oil in a kadhai on medium heat for a few minutes. If the oil is not hot enough, the wadis will turn out greasy. To test the oil, drop a small amount of the leftover paste in – it should sizzle and immediately rise to the surface. Once the oil is hot enough, carefully fry the pieces until golden-brown and crispy on both sides.

For added flavour, you can add a tempered mixture. For this, heat oil in a small pan on medium heat for a few seconds, then add rai and til. Allow the seeds to splutter, then remove from heat and pour the tempered oil over the fried wadis.

Enjoy the crispy wadis hot with a chutney of your choice.

5 alu (colocasia leaves)

60g (2oz) besan (gram flour)

30g (1oz) rice flour

salt, to taste

½ tsp haldi (turmeric powder)

1 tsp lal mirch (red chilli powder)

½ tsp dhaniya (coriander powder)

½ tsp jeera (cumin) powder

1 tbsp tamarind extract

1 tbsp jaggery

500ml (17fl oz) oil

For tempering (optional)

½ tbsp oil

1 tsp rai (mustard seeds)

1 tsp til (sesame seeds)

Seasonal special | Serves 3 | Prep 40 minutes | Cook 35 minutes

Ambadi bhaji

A Maharashtrian special made with roselle leaves, the queen of the monsoon greens

Drain all the soaked ingredients and set aside. Discard the water.

In a saucepan, boil 250ml (8½fl oz) of water, then add the chopped ambadi leaves and cook until they wilt slightly. Remove the leaves, discard the water, and set aside. You know, boiling the leaves can actually take away their sourness.

In a pressure cooker, combine the soaked toor dal, rice, peanuts, and cooked ambadi leaves with 250ml (8½fl oz) of water. Secure the lid and bring to full pressure on medium heat, for 20 minutes. Remove from heat and allow the pressure to release naturally before removing the lid.

Next, in a large pan, heat 2 tablespoons of oil and add rai. When the seeds start to splutter, add hing and the crushed garlic cloves and let it sizzle. Then, add haldi and lal mirch, and cook for a few seconds. Add in the pressure-cooked mixture, then stir in jaggery and grated fresh coconut. If the bhaji seems too thick, add a little more water. Season with salt and cook until well combined.

In a small pan, heat ½ tablespoon of oil and add sookhi lal mirch. Once they sizzle, pour the tempered mixture over the ambadi bhaji and stir gently to combine.

Enjoy this with a millet bhakri.

bunch of ambadi (roselle) leaves, chopped

1 tbsp toor dal (yellow split peas), soaked in water for 30 minutes

1 tbsp rice, coarsely ground and soaked in water for 30 minutes

2 tbsp peanuts, soaked for 30 minutes

2½ tbsp oil, of which ½ tbsp is for tempering

1 tsp rai (mustard seeds)

¼ tsp hing (asafoetida)

8 garlic cloves, peeled and crushed

¼ tsp haldi (turmeric powder)

¼ tsp lal mirch (red chilli powder)

50g (1¾oz) jaggery

50g (1¾oz) grated fresh coconut

salt, to taste

2 sookhi lal mirch (dried red chillies, whole)

CHANGE OF SEASONS

The trees are with flowers, the waters with lotuses... the wind is fragrant, evenings pleasurable, days charming... dearest, everything is exceedingly beautiful in the spring!

Kalidasa in *Ritusamhara* on spring, or वसंत (vasant)

The earth is rendered white by the Kas grass, the nights by the rays of the Moon, river waters by swans, lakes by white water lilies, forests by the scholar trees weighted down by flowers, and the gardens by jasmine.

Kalidasa in *Ritusamhara* on autumn, or पतझड़ (patajhad)

The period of fasting and feasting

In India, both seasonal changes – from summer to winter and vice versa – are marked by celebrations honouring the divine feminine. Many of these festivals celebrate Mother Earth and acknowledge her role in nurturing all life. They pay tribute to the fundamental forces of nature – earth, water, sky, fire and air – and encourage us to embody their qualities in our lives.

The essence of these celebrations lies in integrating staple foods and wild ingredients. As the seasons change, embracing a balance between these elements is crucial. It is not about sticking to purely mass-produced commercial crops or solely wild foods but rather incorporating a diverse mix of both to ensure a well-rounded diet.

Fasting practices in these celebrations highlight the diversity in food as they introduce dishes that are not part of our regular diet. For instance, during this time, there is a focus on consuming legumes, root vegetables, and millets – foods that are often forgotten in daily meals.

Ber, the wild fruit

One such ingredient is ber (Indian jujube), a wild fruit. Sellers commonly stock this fruit around Vasant Panchami, a festival that marks the arrival of spring, after the chill of winters, and in honour of Saraswati, the goddess of knowledge and wisdom. Ber is the traditional *prasad* (offering) for Saraswati. Unlike cultivated fruits typically offered to deities such as bananas, mangoes, and coconuts – fruits that require careful nurturing and specific protocols for watering and care – ber grows spontaneously in the wild or along farm boundaries. It thrives without any attention, growing thorny and unkempt. Its wild growth and thorns reflect the lessons one could learn from life's challenges. It embodies the essence of self-reliance and the introspective journey after navigating adversity.

In Maharashtra, the humble ber plays a central role in a unique tradition known as "*bor nahan*", which means "bathe in berries". It involves bathing a child in ber around the age of two. But the practice holds deeper health significance beyond its festive nature. Ber is a highly nutritious fruit, rich in vitamin C, antioxidants, and various other nutrients. It provides health benefits that many other fruits do not, such as boosting immunity. Its slightly tart and sour flavour may not be particularly appealing to a young child if eaten directly. Bathing in ber allows the child to familiarize and celebrate the connection with this fruit. Over time this helps in cultivating a taste for the fruit and benefitting from its nutritional properties without having to consume the fruit directly.

Nine days of Navratri

Navratri, celebrated when the seasons change, honours the Goddess. While spring signifies new and young love, autumn is about enduring and mature love. The festivals in these periods also mark the same qualities. The Chaitra Navratri, held in March and/or April, marks the onset of summer. Spring is all about fresh beginnings, and local foods play a big role. People enjoy sherbets made from bel (wood apple) and phalsa (Indian summer berry). In some regions, chutneys made from neem leaves are had as a detox of sorts, the bitter pill of nature for sweet beginnings. In Maharashtra, the focus shifts to Gudi Padwa, a spring festival that heralds the Marathi and Konkani New Year, or the Hindu New Year.

On the other hand, the Sharad Navratri, which takes place in September and/or October, precedes winter and is celebrated extensively in the west and the south. This is a time for vibrant cultural activities, late-night communal dancing, and feasting. In recent years, an intriguing trend has emerged in Mumbai during Navratri – commuters on trains coordinate their attire according to a specific colour announced for the day. This colourful tradition adds a fun element to the festival and promotes a sense of unity. Additionally, this practice of synchronized dressing can be seen as a way to enhance collective spirit and bolster community cohesion.

Gudi padwa celebration at home

Fasting foods – (clockwise from top) sweet potato, banana chips, vari tandul, danyachi amti, sabudana khichdi, and rajgeera puri

Fasting practices and traditions, however, are different across the country, particularly regarding the consumption of legumes. In Maharashtra and south India, during the Haldi-Kumkum tradition of Chaitra Navratri, married women visit each other's homes in the evening to participate in rituals involving the application of haldi (turmeric) and kumkum (vermilion powder). Ambe dal (see pp218–19) and aam panna (a traditional raw mango drink) are popular foods during this celebration. If it is Sharad Navratri, they also eat sundal, made from boiled legumes and seasoned with spices. In fact, in the South, sundal is a preferred snack made each evening during Navratri.

On the last day of the festival, the focus shifts from legumes to puri (deep-fried flatbread) with shrikhand (a sweet yogurt-based dish). In contrast, in north India, legumes prominently feature on the last day of Navratri, typically in the form of chana puri (spiced chickpeas with deep-fried bread) and halwa (a semolina-based sweet) as *prasad* while the other days may have been spent fasting on fruits or buckwheat or vari tandul (see pp166).

Food practices vary as well. During Chaitra Navratri, many local fruits and flowers are in season, therefore, there is a greater emphasis on using ingredients such as kaccha keri (raw mango) and legumes, resulting in dishes that often require minimal cooking and incorporate more water. In contrast, during Sharad Navratri, less fresh produce is in season, so milk and other dairy products become more prominent in the diet. This return to dairy products also reflects the cyclical nature of seasonal transitions and the importance of maintaining dietary diversity.

Fasting food

In north India and several other Indian states, including Maharashtra, it is common to eat root vegetables during fasting periods. This practice is about enhancing the diversity by including foods that are not regularly a part of one's diet. As a result, cooking often shifts to dishes featuring yams, sweet potatoes, and arbi (taro root). Some of these root vegetables are wild and less frequently consumed. But

Puran poli with ghee

they come in various colours such as purple, brown, and yellow, adding diversity to the diet. These root vegetables provide nutrients that are typically less available in a regular diet. At a molecular level, they contain nutrients beneficial for hormonal health.

Incorporating these vegetables also introduces new ways of cooking that might not be part of everyday practices, for example, steaming with salt and spices and cooking in earthen pots, or even underground in some regions. Often, when these traditional practices fall out of use, the vegetables associated with them also disappear from forests and farms. When cuisine is no longer practised the traditional way, the wisdom to recognize the wild vegetables when they grow in season, the diversity of crops and seeds, and the entire wealth of "soil to soul" and connection of people to farms and forests is lost.

Dairy products are also allowed during fasting. While this may make the meal seem heavy on calories, consuming more milk and dairy products provides additional amino acids. This approach helps achieve a balanced diet, as it includes a variety of foods to ensure nutritional balance. It is also important to remember that at one time in India, women had access to certain "heavy" foods only during fasts – on regular days, it was always the men who had the first right over resources.

Fasting during Navratri comes to a close with Dussehra, which celebrates the triumph of good over evil. This marks the beginning of the season for hearty dishes such as dal baati (spiced lentil stew and bread) and shrikhand and puri (sweet yogurt with deep-fried flatbread). These heavy dishes are part of the seasonal transitions because they ensure that calorie intake remains sufficient to ward off infections and flu that can arise from a reduced diet due to the week-long fasting period.

Local produce at the market

In honour of the Moon

Festivals celebrated towards summer honour the Sun, while those towards winter honour the Moon. In north India, one such festival is Karva Chauth, celebrated on the fourth day after the full moon in the Hindu month of Kartika (usually October or November). As with many festivals during this transitional period, fasting plays a central role. A full-day fast is broken only after sighting the Moon and completing a series of rituals that include prayers for marital happiness and prosperity.

In Maharashtra, the Moon is celebrated through Kojagiri Purnima. This celebration compares one's love to the gentle light of the Moon, which offers a cool, soothing ambiance, unlike other lights that provide warmth. The idea is that true love, like moonlight, brings comfort and serenity. However, unlike Karva Chauth, which is centred around married couples, Kojagiri is about the community. People come together at night to sing and dance, and celebrations culminate in drinking milk that has been kept under the moonlight and infused with saffron and almonds. It is believed that the Goddess visits each home asking, "*Koja garti*? (who is still awake?)", and those who remain awake are thought to receive blessings of good health and prosperity.

Additionally, in many Indian states, such as Uttar Pradesh, Haryana, Rajasthan, and parts of Gujarat, people celebrate a festival called Sheetla Ashtami, also known as Basoda, eight days after Holi, the festival of colours. This unique festival involves refraining from cooking and instead consuming cold, *baasi* (stale) food. It marks a final farewell to the remnants of winter and the transition into summer.

Eating local

There is a common misconception that we are gaining weight simply because we are burning fewer calories than before. However, this view lacks scientific depth. We do not have data on calorie expenditure from 400–500 years ago because measurements were not recorded at that time. And, even though the available data shows that there has been a marked increase in sedentary lifestyle from the 1950s onwards, interestingly, calorie expenditure has remained consistent. That is because a majority of the daily calorie burn comes from basic bodily functions and organ activity, which has not significantly changed. And even though modern improvements in healthcare have reduced the incidence of infections, slightly lowering overall calorie expenditure, nevertheless, this reduction is minimal. The real issue is not a drop in calorie expenditure, but a shift in dietary patterns. As we increasingly consume processed and packaged foods, which are often low in nutrients relative to their calorie content, we face rising obesity rates.

There is also a shift away from our traditional foods towards those that have not been a part of our diet. This shift reflects a broader change in our eating habits, where we have lost quite a lot of the diversity in the foods we consume. Previously, rice was available in numerous varieties, each suited to specific dishes like kheer (rice pudding), biryani, and khichdi (one-pot meal of rice and pulses). Now, there is a reduction not only in the variety of grains but also in the diversity within grains themselves.

The changes in our diet reflect the change in agricultural practices; from a more diverse crop cycle to monocultures. To combat this, we have to focus on bringing back diversity to our plate in the form of local, seasonal, traditional foods.

Summer fruit and flower blossoms

CHANGE OF SEASONS

Rice kheer

For example, during seasonal transitions, include hyperlocal fruits such as jamun (Indian blackberry) and karonda (Bengal currants) into your diet. Jamun can be used to create refreshing beverages, while karonda pairs well with fresh green chillies to make a tangy and spicy accompaniment. Flowers and leaves also have a unique role during change of seasons, adding both flavour and colour to various dishes. Mogra flowers are often used to make fragrant sherbets, while rose petals are crafted into gulkand (a sweet preserve of rose petals). While some flowers are directly incorporated into meals, Indian food traditionally uses fewer flowers. That is because the food is so much about aroma, and the strong scents from flowers can interfere with the eating experience. So, although hibiscus tea and juice have gained popularity on social media, they are not a part of traditional Indian meals.

As the season shifts from Dussehra towards winter, bajra becomes a staple grain, lasting until the spring. By March, the focus shifts to ragi and jowar, while bajra is phased out. During this seasonal change towards winter, people often experience increased hair loss and dandruff. Bajra, rich in iron, helps mitigate these issues by preventing excessive hair fall and dandruff.

"Jamun . . . to create refreshing beverages . . . mogra . . . to make fragrant sherbets, while rose petals . . . into gulkand."

A matter of assimilation

While prioritizing native foods of your region is important, some non-native items have seamlessly integrated into traditional Indian diets. The key is that such foods should not dominate, but should complement existing eating patterns and be versatile enough to be used in several different ways. The challenge arises when non-native foods start displacing native ingredients, disrupting traditional practices and diminishing the role of local foods.

Good examples of non-native foods that have found a place in regional cuisines across India are makhana (fox nut) and sabudana (tapioca pearls), alongside some imports such as rose and cashew. Historically, makhana and sabudana were cultivated to combat diarrhoea and replenish the energy, but nowadays they have become common in many regional diets, particularly during fasting periods.

Although makhana has been a staple in some parts of north India, as a snack, pudding, and even curry, its consumption is steadily growing across the country now. While occasional intake is fine, excessive consumption of makhana can lead to issues such as constipation, especially among people who are less familiar with it and have not traditionally eaten it. This sudden upsurge in makhana consumption is because, in recent years, it has been promoted as a superfood and marketed as a healthy snack and a better alternative to chips. While this is true for makhanas fried in ghee at home, packaged makhana often falls short, not just on nutrition but on authentic taste also.

(From left) A sneak peak into Rujuta's daily meals – soaked raisins and almonds; poha with grated coconut; and rice, green bhaji, peanut chutney, jowar bhakri, and pumpkin raita

Meal planning

Seasonal changes often feel more pronounced with fluctuating temperatures than with the extremes of hot or cold. Therefore, correct meal planning during these transitional periods is crucial to maintain balance and prevent mood swings.

CHANGE OF SEASONS 199

Starting the day with a mix of dry fruits and nuts, such as anjeer (dried fig) or raisins paired with almonds, dates, or walnuts, can help set a balanced tone. For breakfast, maintaining a consistent routine is beneficial. However, lunch should adapt to the seasons – thepla and bhakri (spiced flatbreads) are favoured as winter approaches, while rice-based dishes and refreshing sherbets become more prevalent as summer begins. Dinner routines vary regionally but carry even more weight during the change of season. A hearty dinner will ensure good sleep and digestion, which are often affected during this time.

Millets have traditionally been part of daily meals across the country, before they fell out of favour, especially the smaller millets such as samo (little millet) and kodo (foxtail millet) that were consumed during change of seasons, usually during fasts. Now,

Ratalacha kees

Khichdi with raita

however, millets are making a comeback, and there is a growing trend to replace the regular grains with millets, wholesale. However, a complete shift away from rice and wheat towards millets is not a good idea. There are specific grains and millets for different seasons and occasions and maintaining these variations is crucial.

Adapting your diet to the changing seasons and climate is about maintaining a balanced lifestyle that is in rhythm with nature. Simply consuming nutrient-rich foods out of a greed for their benefits, without considering the right combinations, timing, and proportions, can lead to ineffective digestion and excretion, regardless of how nutritious the food is. So, while incorporating millets into your diet is beneficial, it is important to complement them with other traditional elements, such as ghee, makkhan, and jaggery et cetera. Embracing these foods in their complete, traditional forms ensures that you maximize their benefits and maintain proper balance in your diet.

"Adapting your diet to the changing seasons and climate is about maintaining a balanced lifestyle that is in rhythm with nature."

Seasonal drink | Serves 3 | Prep 15 minutes | Cook 25 minutes

Kulith kalan

Nutritious horse gram drink, perfect for late nights or after parties, and great to enjoy on its own when I am not in the mood for a full lunch

In a pressure cooker, combine 300ml (10fl oz) of water with kulith. Secure the lid and bring to full pressure on medium heat, for 15 minutes. Remove from heat and let the pressure release naturally before opening the cooker. Strain the kulith, reserving the cooking water. Instead of discarding the kulith, you can temper it with basic spices and eat with roti.

Next, in a pan, bring the reserved kulith water to a gentle simmer.

Meanwhile, heat ghee in a small pan on medium heat for a few seconds, and add hing and jeera. When the seeds begin to splutter, add curry leaves and green chillies, and let them sizzle. Pour this tempered mixture over the simmering kulith water and stir well.

Add buttermilk and sugar. Season with salt and mix thoroughly.

Enjoy it while it is steaming hot.

100g (3½oz) kulith (horse gram)

1 tsp ghee

pinch of hing (asafoetida)

½ tsp jeera (cumin seeds)

2 green chillies

4 curry leaves

120ml (4fl oz) buttermilk

½ tsp sugar

salt, to taste

Something sweet | Makes 8 | Prep 15 minutes, plus 1½ hours of soaking and resting | Cook 20 minutes | Special equipment kadhai

Aliv laddoo

Made with garden cress seeds, coconut, and jaggery, these laddoos are the perfect therapy for frizzy hair and dull skin

Drain the coconut water or milk from the soaked aliv. Then, mix in the grated fresh coconut and jaggery. Let it rest for about 30 minutes.

In a kadhai, heat ghee on medium heat for a few seconds. Once hot, add the aliv–coconut–jaggery mixture and cook it, stirring continuously. As it cooks, the jaggery will melt and blend with the coconut, creating a fragrant and sticky mixture. Keep stirring until it thickens and reaches a consistency that can be easily shaped into small balls.

Once the mixture has thickened, remove it from the heat and let it cool slightly. For an added layer of flavour, sprinkle jaiphal powder and stir well to infuse the aroma into the mixture.

Now comes the fun part. Take a handful of the mixture and roll it into small balls between your palms to create laddoos. The warmth from your hands will help shape them perfectly.

Store the laddoos in an airtight container in the fridge. They can be enjoyed for up to a week, making them a convenient and delicious treat to satisfy your sweet cravings any time of the day.

75g (2½oz) aliv (garden cress seeds), soaked in 150ml (5fl oz) of coconut water or milk for 1 hour

75g (2½oz) grated fresh coconut

150g (5¼oz) jaggery

½ tbsp ghee

pinch of jaiphal (nutmeg) powder

Savoury bite | Makes 4 | Prep 45 minutes | Cook 10 minutes |
Special equipment chakla–belan (rolling pin and board) and cast iron tawa

Upvasache thalipeeth

A unique combination of millets and tapioca pearls for all devotees of good taste

To make bhajani, heat a pan on medium heat for about half a minute, then add all the ingredients. Dry roast them, stirring continuously, until they turn golden-brown. Once roasted, transfer the mixture to a plate and let it cool. After cooling, grind it finely using a grinder. This flour can be stored for up to 6 months, thanks to the sookhi lal mirch, which acts as a natural preservative.

To make thalipeeth, in a large bowl combine bhajani, grated red pumpkin, powdered peanuts, chopped green chillies, and salt. If you do not have red pumpkin, you can use a grated potato or raw banana. Gradually add 80ml (2¾fl oz) of water, mixing until you form a soft dough. Once combined, cover the bowl with a cloth and let the dough rest for 15 minutes.

After the dough has rested, pinch off a handful and use chakla–belan to roll it into thin circles. Aim for an even thickness to ensure uniform cooking.

Next, heat a cast iron tawa on medium heat for a few seconds. Spread ½ tablespoon of ghee evenly across the tawa surface and allow it to heat up for a couple of seconds. Once the ghee is hot, gently place the rolled thalipeeth on the tawa. Cover the tawa with a lid and cook one side until it turns a beautiful golden-brown.

Carefully flip the thalipeeth over and cook the other side, without the lid this time, until it develops the same lovely golden colour. Once both sides are perfectly cooked, remove the thalipeeth from the tawa.

Enjoy it hot with home-set dahi (curd) (*see p101*).

For bhajani (flour for thalipeeth)

1.5kg (3lb 3oz) sabudana (tapioca pearls)

1.5kg (3lb 3oz) amaranth seeds

1.5kg (3lb 3oz) vari rice (barnyard millet)

1 tsp jeera (cumin seeds)

5–6 sookhi lal mirch (dried red chillies, whole)

For thalipeeth

120g (4¼oz) bhajani

50g (1¾oz) red pumpkin, peeled and grated

50g (1¾oz) peanuts, powdered

2 green chillies, finely chopped

salt, to taste

2 tbsp ghee, ½ tbsp for each thalipeeth

Accompaniment | **Makes** 350g (12¼oz) | **Prep** 3 days | **Cook** 20 minutes

Mango pickle

My mother's version of a classic Indian recipe

Pickles in India are an emotion rooted in family tradition and a staple side in most of my meals. This one takes 3 days to make.

Day 1
Heat a pan on medium heat for a few seconds and dry roast the sendha namak until all moisture is gone. Then, in a glass bowl, combine the diced, sun-dried raw mangoes with 1 teaspoon of haldi and the roasted namak. Allow the mixture to sit overnight to enhance the flavours.

Day 2
In a small pan, heat ½ tablespoon of mustard oil on medium heat for a few seconds and fry methi until crispy. Remove from heat and let it cool, then crush it into a fine powder. If you prefer a mildly bitter pickle, you can reduce the amount of methi.

Add 1 tablespoon of powdered rai, the crushed methi, and lal mirch to the raw mangoes and mix well to combine. You can adjust the quantity of lal mirch to your taste and also add Kashmiri lal mirch, which adds a vibrant colour without the spiciness. Let it sit overnight.

Day 3
In a pan, heat the remaining mustard oil on medium heat until it begins to smoke. Heating it properly mellows its pungent flavour. Next, add rai 2 tablespoons of rai and once the seeds start to splutter, stir in hing and ½ teaspoon of haldi. Remove the pan from heat and let it cool to room temperature. Once cooled, pour it over the spiced raw mangoes. If needed, add more oil to ensure it floats above the mango pieces.

You can store this mango pickle in an airtight container for up to 3 months and enjoy as an accompaniment to any meal.

- 3 tbsp sendha namak (rock salt)
- 2 raw mangoes, diced and sun-dried for 1 hour
- 1½ tsp haldi (turmeric powder), of which ½ tsp is for tempering
- 180ml (6fl oz) mustard oil, of which ½ tbsp is for frying methi
- 2 tsp methi (fenugreek seeds)
- 3 tbsp rai (mustard seeds), of which 1 tbsp is powdered
- ½ tbsp lal mirch (red chilli powder)
- 1–2 tsp Kashmiri lal mirch (Kashmiri red chilli powder), optional
- 1 tsp hing (asafoetida)

Mango pickle

Everyday meal | **Serves** 3 | **Prep** 15 minutes | **Cook** 25 minutes |
Special equipment kadhai and hand blender

Dal and bhaat

If there is a meal that embodies the essence of Indian food, it is this one – fueling you with power for 24 hours

Heat oil in a kadhai on medium heat for a few seconds. Once the oil is hot, add rai. When the seeds begin to splutter, add hing and curry leaves. Allow the leaves to sizzle. Stir in the spices – lal mirch, haldi, and dhaniya – sauté them for a few seconds until the oil is infused with their flavour.

Now, add the pressure-cooked dal along with 350ml (12fl oz) of water. Mix everything together until well combined. Use a hand blender to churn the mixture until it is mashed. If you like the dal to have some texture, you can skip this step.

Next, add the kokum for tanginess, followed by the grated fresh coconut. Season with salt.

Stir gently to mix everything together. Let the dal simmer on low heat for about 10 minutes, allowing the flavours to develop and meld beautifully.

Enjoy the dal with steaming hot rice (*see p159*).

100g (3½oz) toor dal, pressure cooked

½ tbsp oil

½ tsp rai (mustard seeds)

pinch of hing (asafoetida)

5–6 curry leaves

½ tsp lal mirch (red chilli powder)

½ tsp haldi (turmeric powder)

½ tsp dhaniya (coriander powder)

1 kokum

½ tbsp grated fresh coconut

salt, to taste

Rice dish | Makes 3 | Prep time 20 minutes, plus 1 hour of resting | Cook 15 minutes | Special equipment iron or cast iron tawa

Amboli

These thin, crisp pancakes are a must-try Konkan dish

Grind rice, chana dal, urad dal, dhaniya seeds, and methi together in a grinder to create the blended flour for amboli. You can store it in an airtight glass container.

Now, we will make the batter. In a bowl, mix 150ml (5fl oz) of water with dahi to make instant buttermilk. Alternatively, you can use the buttermilk leftover from churning dahi into butter. Gradually add this mixture to the amboli flour, stirring well to eliminate any lumps. Allow the batter to rest for 1 hour.

After resting, season the batter with lal mirch, haldi, and salt, then fold in crushed garlic cloves.

Heat an iron or cast iron tawa on medium heat for a few seconds. Add 1 tablespoon of ghee and spread it evenly across the surface of the tawa.

Pour a generous spoonful of the batter onto the tawa, then use the back of a ladle to evenly spread it out into a thin layer, and cover with a lid. Cook on low heat until one side is set, then flip the amboli and cook for a couple more minutes until golden.

Serve hot with ghee.

150g (5¼oz) rice, preferably patni variety

30g (1oz) chana dal (split Bengal gram)

15g (½oz) urad dal (black gram)

20g (¾oz) dhaniya (coriander) seeds

1 tsp methi (fenugreek seeds)

100g (3½oz) home-set dahi (curd)

½ tsp lal mirch (red chilli powder)

½ tsp haldi (turmeric powder)

salt, to taste

4 garlic cloves, peeled and crushed

3 tbsp ghee, 1 tbsp for each amboli

Millet prep | Serves 3 | Prep 15 minutes | Cook 45 minutes | Special equipment tawa

Pithla and bhakri

Maharashtra's most practical and spiritual meal, a perfect choice for last-minute guests

For the pithla, heat oil in a pan on medium heat for a few seconds. Once the oil is hot, add rai and let the seeds splutter. Now add the chopped garlic clove, curry leaves, and lal mirch. Cook for a few seconds so that the oil absorbs all those flavours. Add the chopped onion and season with salt and haldi. Cook until the onion turns soft and translucent.

While the onion is cooking, whisk together besan and 250ml (8½fl oz) of water in a separate bowl. Do not worry if the consistency is too thin.

Next, pour the whisked mixture into the pan and cook, stirring occasionally, until it thickens to a creamy consistency. Garnish with fresh coriander leaves and enjoy with bhakri.

For the bhakri, in a bowl, combine rice flour and salt. Gradually add 80ml (2¾fl oz) of warm water, kneading as you go, until it becomes a soft, pliable dough. Since you are using rice flour, the dough will be slightly looser compared to one made with wholewheat flour.

For pithla

1 tbsp oil

½ tsp rai (mustard seeds)

1 garlic clove, peeled and chopped

5 curry leaves

¼ tsp lal mirch (red chilli powder)

1 onion, peeled and chopped

salt, to taste

¼ tsp haldi (turmeric powder)

60g (2oz) besan (gram flour)

fresh coriander leaves, for garnish

Take a small portion of the dough and roll it into a ball between your palms. Then, flatten it out with your palms to form thin discs. Repeat with the remaining dough.

Heat a tawa on medium heat for a few seconds. Place each disc on the tawa and roast it on both sides until golden and crisp.

Serve hot with pithla for a delightful meal. What makes bhakri unique is that it can be enjoyed both hot and cold. The leftover bhakri from dinner are great for breakfast the next day. I simply spread ghee over it and eat it with a peanut chutney (see p114).

For bhakri

120g (4¼oz) rice flour

½ tsp salt

Isn't it incredible how dishes like ambe dal can carry so much meaning?

The dishes closest to our hearts are often the ones that remind us of our loved ones. Ambe dal is like that. It takes me back to my aaji. While the recipe has just a few ingredients, what makes it special is that it is mixed by hand. At least that's how my aaji would make it.

What is truly special about dishes like ambe dal is how they are crafted to meet the needs of all age groups. Ambe dal uses pulses to enhance raw mango, which is not always palatable given its sharp sourness, especially for older people. But when it is incorporated into ambe dal, it retains its tangy flavour without overwhelming the tongue or causing discomfort to the teeth. Ambe dal is truly a reflection of the wisdom passed down through generations.

Traditional taste | **Serves** 2 | **Prep** 30 minutes, plus 4–5 hours of soaking | **Cook** 5 minutes | **Special equipment** mortar and pestle

Ambe dal

My maternal grandmother's signature dish still brings a wave of warmth and nostalgia every time I have it

Drain the chana dal and set it aside. In a mortar, add jeera, green chilli, and 2 curry leaves. Use a pestle to grind them coarsely. Once ground, transfer the mixture to a bowl.

Add the grated raw mango for a tangy kick and season with salt. Toss in some grated fresh coconut for a bit of sweetness and texture, and sugar to balance the flavours. Mix everything thoroughly so that the ingredients are well combined.

Next, heat oil in a pan on medium heat for just a few seconds. Add rai and let the seeds splutter. Then, add hing, sookhi lal mirch, haldi, and the remaining curry leaves. Sauté the spices for a minute or so until they release their aromatic flavours.

Pour this sizzling tempering over the dal mixture in the bowl. Stir everything together gently. Finally, garnish with fresh coriander leaves and enjoy with family and friends.

100g (3½oz) chana dal (split Bengal gram), soaked in water for 4–5 hours

½ tsp jeera (cumin seeds)

1 green chilli

5 curry leaves, of which 3 are for tempering

½ raw mango, peeled and grated

salt, to taste

1 tbsp grated fresh coconut

½ tsp sugar

1 tbsp oil

½ tsp rai (mustard seeds)

½ tsp hing (asafoetida)

2 sookhi lal mirch (dried red chillies, whole)

¼ tsp haldi (turmeric powder)

fresh coriander leaves, for garnish

Seasonal special | Serves 2 | Prep 45 minutes | Cook 25 minutes

Banana flower sabzi

Made with banana blossoms and often used as traditional remedy for improving hormonal balance and reducing acne and stretch marks

Peel off the outer maroon leaves of the banana flower and discard them. Don't worry, these leaves are inedible. Once you have removed those, you will find a row of smaller florets at the base, which are the tasty parts we want to use. But before cooking, we will need to do a little prep work. It is a bit of effort, but trust me, it is worth it for the delicious flavour.

For each floret, we need to remove two inedible parts. First, locate the stamen, which is situated in the centre of the floret and appears as a long filament with a tiny bulb at the tip. Carefully grasp it and pull it out. Next, look for a thin, plastic-like flap near the base of the floret. Gently peel this away and discard it as well. Repeat this process for each floret until you reach the solid white core, which is perfectly safe to eat. Now, chop the florets and the white part finely. Then, soak the pieces in buttermilk and set aside – this helps prevent discolouration while you prepare the rest of the dish.

In a pressure cooker, heat oil on medium heat for a few seconds and then add rai. Once the seeds begin to splutter, stir in hing and haldi and sauté for a few seconds until fragrant. Next, add chopped green chillies for a hint of heat.

Strain the soaked banana flower and add it to the cooker, along with drained peanuts and jaggery. Stir everything together to ensure it is well combined. Then, incorporate lal mirch, goda masala, and salt. Mix thoroughly. Instead of soaked peanuts, you can also use soaked red chana (red chickpeas), sprouted moong dal (green gram), or even cashews.

Now, secure the lid of the pressure cooker and cook on medium heat until it reaches full pressure, for 20 minutes. Allow the pressure to release naturally, then carefully remove the lid. Give it a good stir and let it simmer for an additional 10 minutes to meld the flavours.

Finally, garnish with grated fresh coconut and serve hot.

1 banana flower

250ml (8½fl oz) buttermilk

2 tbsp oil

½ tsp rai (mustard seeds)

pinch of hing (asafoetida)

½ tsp haldi (turmeric powder)

2–3 green chillies, finely chopped

1 tbsp peanuts, soaked in water for 10 minutes

2 tbsp jaggery

1 tsp lal mirch (red chilli powder)

1 tsp goda masala (Maharashtrian spice mix)

salt, to taste

grated fresh coconut, for garnish

Unique prep | **Serves** 2 | **Prep** 10 minutes | **Cook** 20 minutes

White pumpkin halwa

A testament that pumpkin is anything but boring

With your hands, squeeze out all the excess water from the grated pumpkin. Mix the grated pumpkin with sugar – you can adjust the sweetness to your liking by increasing the amount of sugar.

Now, heat a pan on medium heat for a few seconds and add the pumpkin–sugar mixture. Cook it, while stirring frequently, until it thickens and becomes almost dry – but be careful not to let it dry out completely.

Once the mixture has reached the right consistency, stir in jaiphal or elaichi powder for aroma. Add chopped nuts and raisins for added texture. Mix everything well.

Enjoy 2–3 tablespoons of this halwa everyday to boost your immunity. Savour it on its own or pair with roti.

500g (1lb 2oz) white pumpkin, peeled and grated

100g (3½oz) sugar

pinch of jaiphal (nutmeg) powder, or elaichi (cardamom) powder

4 almonds, chopped

4 cashews, chopped

1 tbsp raisins

Something sweet | Makes 6 | Prep 30 minutes, plus 2 hours of resting | Cook 20 minutes

Rava–nariyal laddoo

Perfect treat for mood fluctuations and an excellent choice for women going through prolonged periods lasting over 10 days

In a heavy-based pan, heat 3 tablespoons of ghee on low heat for a few seconds. Add rava and roast it, stirring continuously to ensure even cooking and to prevent it from burning. Soon, you will start to see ghee clinging to your spatula, but if it seems a bit dry, add a little more ghee.

When the rava feels lighter and has turned light golden-brown in colour, add the grated nariyal to the pan. Continue to roast this mixture, stirring regularly, until the aroma fills the room. This is a key indicator that the rava and nariyal are perfectly roasted. Once done, remove the mixture from the heat and transfer it to a plate. It is essential not to leave it in the hot pan as it will continue to cook and may burn.

Next, in a separate pan, combine sugar and 125ml (4½fl oz) of water. Cook this mixture on medium heat until you see bubbles forming across the entire surface of the pan. To check for the correct consistency, dip two fingers into the syrup, quickly take them out and pull apart – you should see a taar (single string) forming between your fingers. This indicates that the syrup is ready. But be careful as the syrup will be hot. Remove it from the heat and carefully mix in the roasted rava–nariyal mixture.

Stir in elaichi powder for a fragrant touch and add raisins for a bit of sweetness and texture. Cover the pan with a lid and let it cool for a couple of hours. This resting period allows the flavours to meld beautifully.

After the mixture has cooled, it is time to shape the laddoos. Grease your palms with 1 tablespoon of ghee to prevent sticking. Then, take small portions of the mixture and roll into small balls between your palms. If you find that the mixture is too dry and crumbly, simply add a bit more ghee. Place the laddoos on a plate and let them set.

Enjoy them immediately or store in an airtight container for later.

4 tbsp ghee, of which 1 tbsp is for greasing

175g (6oz) rava (semolina), half fine-grained and half coarse-grained varieties

125g (4½oz) grated nariyal (fresh coconut)

150g (5¼oz) sugar

pinch of elaichi (cardamom) powder

8–10 raisins

Traditional taste | Serves 2 | **Prep** 10 minutes, plus 12–14 hours of setting and draining | **Cook** 15 minutes | **Special equipment** cheesecloth/muslin cloth and puran yantra (optional)

Shrikhand

A hung curd delicacy that you must eat atleast once a year

In a saucepan, heat milk on low heat for 10–12 minutes. Be sure to leave the malai (cream) intact. Just before the milk comes to boil, add buttermilk and stir. If you do not have buttermilk, simply mix 1 teaspoon of home-set dahi (curd) with 1 tablespoon of water for an instant version. Pour this mixture into a bowl and let it set for 7–8 hours to make dahi.

Once set, tie the dahi in cheesecloth/muslin cloth and hang it for 5–6 hours to allow the water to drain, resulting in chakka (hung curd).

Next, mix powdered sugar into the chakka. Place this mixture in a strainer and gently stir with your hand, allowing the shrikhand to drip into a bowl below. Alternatively, you can use a puran yantra, a special masher, for this step.

For flavour, add jaiphal powder and soaked kesar to the shrikhand and mix well.

Finally, garnish with the chopped nuts and enjoy it cold.

- 500ml (17fl oz) full-fat milk
- 1½ tbsp buttermilk
- 100g (3½oz) sugar, powdered
- ¼ tsp jaiphal (nutmeg) powder
- 4–5 kesar (saffron strands), soaked in 1 tbsp of warm milk for 30 minutes
- 1 tbsp pistachios, chopped
- 1 tbsp cashews, chopped

Seasonal special | Serves 3 | Prep 10 minutes | Cook 30 minutes

Kantola vegetable

The cousin of karela who is not bitter about being small

In a pan, heat oil on medium heat for a few seconds. Add rai and once the seeds begin to splutter, add hing and haldi.

Next, add the chopped onion and sauté until it becomes soft and translucent. Then, add the kantola pieces and stir-fry for about a minute to ensure that the kantola is well coated with the masala. Cover the pan with a lid and cook until the pieces are tender, stirring occasionally.

Once the kantola is soft, add lal mirch, dhaniya, jeera powder, salt, and sugar. Stir well and fry for a few more minutes, allowing the spices to blend beautifully.

Finally, garnish with grated fresh coconut and chopped fresh coriander. Serve hot with bhakri or roti.

2 tsp oil

¼ tsp rai (mustard seeds)

⅓ tsp hing (asafoetida)

½ tsp haldi (turmeric powder)

1 onion, peeled and chopped

250g (8¾oz) kantola (spiny gourd), peeled and cut lengthwise

¼ tsp lal mirch (red chilli powder)

½ tsp dhaniya (coriander powder)

½ tsp jeera (cumin) powder

salt, to taste

½ tsp sugar

grated fresh coconut, for garnish

fresh coriander, chopped, for garnish

Savoury bite | Makes 4 | Prep 50 minutes | Cook 10 minutes | **Special equipment** iron or cast iron tawa

Besan cheela

It is the quick fix for when your stomach's rumbling but you don't feel like cooking a masterpiece

In a bowl, combine semolina, besan, dahi, chopped green chillies, chopped fresh coriander, grated ginger, and salt. Add 150ml (5fl oz) of water and mix thoroughly until you achieve a smooth, slightly thick batter that is flowy but not overly liquid. Let the batter rest for at least 30 minutes. This allows the ingredients to meld and the flours to absorb the water.

Once rested, fold in the grated bottle gourd or red pumpkin and mix well.

Next, heat a cast iron or iron tawa on medium heat for a few seconds and add ½ tablespoon of oil, spreading it to create a thin layer. Pour a generous spoonful of the batter onto the tawa and spread it out evenly. Cover the tawa with a lid and cook until the cheela is set. Carefully flip it over and cook the other side until golden-brown, leaving the lid off this time.

Enjoy the cheelas hot with a chutney of your choice.

40g (1½oz) semolina

120g (4¼oz) besan (gram flour)

3 tbsp home-set dahi (curd)

2 green chillies, finely chopped

sprig of fresh coriander, finely chopped

1½cm (½in) fresh ginger, peeled and grated

salt, to taste

60g (2oz) bottle gourd, or red pumpkin, peeled and grated

2 tbsp oil, ½ tbsp for each cheela

GLOSSARY

A

Aaji Marathi term for grandmother
Achar Pickled condiment made from vegetables and fruits, preserved in oil and salt, and seasoned with spices such as mustard and fenugreek
Aga Khan Title held by the spiritual leader of the Ismaili Shia Muslim community
Aliv Garden cress seeds, also known as halim or chandrashoor
Alu Colocasia leaves, commonly used to make crispy fritters
Amaranth Gluten-free grain with a nutty, earthy flavour and subtle peppery kick, which can be used whole or turned into flour
Ambadi Tender leaves of the hibiscus plant, also known as roselle or gongura
Amla Indian gooseberry, a fruit rich in vitamin C and antioxidants, often used in chutneys, pickles, or drinks
Amti Traditional Maharashtrian curry, typically made with lentils and flavoured with goda masala, tamarind, and jaggery
Antioxidants Molecules that prevent or slow down damage to cells caused by free, unstable radicals
Avalokiteshvara Bodhisattva of compassion in Mahayana Buddhism
Ayurvedic Relating to Ayurveda, the traditional system of medicine from India

B

Baarish Rains or the monsoon season in India
Bajra Pearl millet, a staple grain in India during the winter season
Banana flower Flower of the banana plant, commonly used in curries and stews, and known for its slightly bitter flavour
Besan Gram flour, made from chickpeas, commonly used in Indian cooking to make fritters and for thickening gravies
Bhaat Vernacular term for boiled rice
Bhajani Roasted flour mix used in Maharashtra to prepare dishes like bhakri and thalipeeth
Bhaji Marathi term for a vegetable dish or stir-fry, typically prepared with simple spices
Bhajia Deep-fried fritters, made from gram flour and vegetables such as spinach or onion, often served as a snack
Bhakri Type of unleavened flatbread made from various flours such as bajra or jowar
Bhakti movement Religious and social movement, popular between the 15th and 17th centuries, that emphasized devotion to a personal god. It influenced many parts of Maharashtra, particularly through saints such as Sant Tukaram and Dnyaneshwar
Brahmanda The concept of the universe in Hindu cosmology, often discussed in spiritual contexts
Brass Metal often used in traditional kitchenware, including pots, pans, and utensils, in Indian households
Buttermilk Dairy drink made by churning curd with water; also known as chhaas

C

Cast iron Type of cookware, including griddles, used in Indian kitchens for slow cooking
Chaat A popular category of street food in India, characterized by tangy, spicy, and sweet flavours
Chaitra Navratri Festival celebrating the feminine divine, observed in the month of Chaitra (March–April)
Chakla–belan Board and rolling pin used in Indian kitchens, especially for rolling dough to make rotis, puris, and other flatbreads
Chana dal Split and hulled yellow lentils from mature chickpeas
Chaturmasya Period of four months in the Hindu calendar when certain dietary and spiritual practices are observed, often including fasting or vegetarianism
Cheela Savoury pancake made from gram flour or a dal, popular as a breakfast dish or snack
Chhole Chickpeas, a type of legume known for their firm texture and nutty flavour
Chopped Ingredients cut into small pieces, commonly used for preparing vegetables and herbs in cooking
Churmura Puffed rice, commonly used to make tea-time snacks or eaten on its own with spices
Chutney Condiment made from fruits, vegetables, or herbs, mixed with spices; often served alongside main dishes
Cold-pressed Method of extracting oils by pressing the seeds without heat to preserve nutrients and flavour
Creepers Climbing plants or vines, such as gourds, that grow along the ground or up structures
Curry leaves An aromatic herb used for tempering

D

Dahi Traditional Indian yogurt, made by fermenting milk, enjoyed either savoury or sweet
Dals Lentils, covering many varieties like toor, moong, and masoor, often cooked in a spiced curry
Dhana jiru Spice blend of coriander seeds and cumin seeds
Dhaniya Coriander, used fresh as a garnish, or in seed or powdered form as a spice
Dhrupad A classical style of Indian music, often performed in spiritual contexts
Diwali Festival of lights, one of the most significant Hindu celebrations, marking the return of Lord Rama from exile
Dough Mixture of flour, water, and other ingredients used to make flatbreads
Dussehra Hindu festival celebrating the victory of good over evil, observed after the nine days of Navratri

E

Elaichi Cardamom, a fragrant spice used in both sweet and savoury dishes

F

Fasting Voluntary abstention from certain foods, often observed during religious festivals such as Navratri
Fibre An essential nutrient found in fruits, vegetables, grains, and legumes that aids digestion
Fresh coconut Also known as nariyal, it is the brown, hairy stage of the coconut – it has a fibrous outer shell and a sweet, white inner flesh that can be eaten raw or used in cooking

G

Ganesha Chaturthi A major festival in Maharashtra celebrating the birth of Lord Ganesha, the elephant-headed god, marked by processions and offerings of sweets like modaks
Garmi Hot or summer season in India
Garnish Decorative addition to a dish, often using herbs such as fresh coriander, that enhances the visual appeal and flavour of the food
Gauri Ganpati Festival to celebrate Goddess Gauri, believed to be Lord Ganesha's mother
Ghee Clarified butter, commonly used for tempering or added to dishes for its rich, nutty flavour and aroma
Glycemic index Measure of how quickly foods raise blood sugar levels
Goda masala Signature spice blend in Maharashtrian cuisine, typically consisting of roasted spices such as cinnamon, cloves, cardamom, and cumin
Grated Finely shredded ingredients
Greasing Process of applying oil to a pan or palms to prevent sticking
Gudi Padwa Marathi New Year, celebrated by hoisting a gudi (a decorated bamboo stick) in front of homes. It marks the start of the new harvest season

H

Haemoglobin Protein in red blood cells that carries oxygen
Haldi Turmeric, used widely in Indian cuisine for its colour and health benefits
Haldi–Kumkum Tradition where married women offer haldi (turmeric) and kumkum (vermilion) to other women, symbolizing blessings, good health, and prosperity
Halwa Sweet dish made from various ingredients such as carrots, lentils, or semolina, cooked with ghee, sugar, and milk
Hara chana Green, tender chickpeas
Hing Asafoetida, known for its smell and taste, and often used in tempering dals, curries, and pickles
Holi Festival celebrating the arrival of spring, marked by the throwing of coloured powders

J

Jaggery Traditional unrefined sugar made from sugarcane or palm sap
Jaiphal Nutmeg, a spice used in small quantities to add warmth and depth to dishes, particularly in desserts and beverages
Jaman Curd culture used to inoculate milk, allowing it to set into fresh curd
Jeera Cumin seeds, a spice used in tempering or ground into powder for seasoning dishes
Jowar Sorghum, a gluten-free grain used to make flatbreads

K

Kaap Traditional Marathi dish of fried, spiced vegetables
Kadhai Deep, round cooking vessel used for frying or preparing curries
Kadhi Curd-based curry, often served with rice, popular in Marathi and Gujarati cuisine
Kala namak Black salt, a type of rock salt which is considered rich in minerals
Kalan Seasoned stock made from pulses, often enjoyed as an appetizer
Kali mirch Black pepper, used as a spice for its pungency in both savoury and sweet dishes
Kalidasa Ancient Indian poet and playwright, known for works such as *Shakuntala* and *Meghdoot*
Kantola Spiny gourd, resembling bitter gourd but smaller and milder in taste, without the bitterness
Kartika Month in the Hindu lunar calendar, typically occurring in October–November
Karva Chauth Fasting festival celebrated by married women in some parts of India, for the well-being and longevity of their husbands
Kashmiri lal mirch Variety of red chilli pepper from Kashmir, known for its vibrant colour and mild heat
Khadi shakkar Unrefined sugar made from palm sap, similar to jaggery
Kheer Dessert made from milk, rice or millet, and sugar or jaggery
Khichdi One-pot dish made with rice and lentils, often spiced lightly
Kneading Process of working dough by hand
Kojagiri Purnima Festival observed on the full moon night in the month of Ashvin (usually September or October), during which women fast and worship the Moon
Kokanastha Brahmin community Sub-group of Brahmins primarily from the Konkan region of Maharashtra
Kokum Fruit commonly used in coastal Maharashtra for its sourness
Kokum agal Syrup or extract made from kokum – the fruit is dried and then soaked in water to extract its tangy, slightly sweet flavour
Konkan Coastal region in western India, which stretches along the Arabian Sea
Koshimbir Marathi term for salad
Kothimbir Marathi term for coriander leaves

L

Laddoos Sweet, round treats made from various ingredients, bound together with ghee or sugar syrup
Lahasun Garlic, known for its strong flavour and often used in tempering or ground into a paste for curries
Lal mirch Red chilli powder, used to add heat and spice to dishes
Lama Buddhist monk or spiritual

teacher, often associated with Tibetan Buddhism
Lauki Bottle gourd, a mild-flavoured vegetable used in curries
Laung Cloves, aromatic flower buds used as a spice in cooking and in tempering to add warmth and aroma to dishes
Legumes Family of plants that produce seeds in pods, including beans, lentils, and peas, and considered important protein sources
Lentils Dals, used in various forms – either boiled or ground into pastes – to make curries and soups

M

Mahabharata One of the two major Sanskrit epics of ancient India, alongside the *Ramayana*
Malai Cream, the rich part of milk
Malnutrition Condition caused by a deficiency or imbalance of nutrients, which can result from poor diet
Manjushri Bodhisattva of wisdom in Mahayana Buddhism
Marathi Language spoken by people in the state of Maharashtra
Marwari Community originally from Rajasthan, known for their distinct cuisine that uses ghee, gram flour, and spices
Masala Generic term to refer to a mixture of spices, either whole or ground
Meghdoot Sanskrit play by the classical poet Kalidasa
Methi Fenugreek, both the seeds and the fresh leaves
Micronutrients Vitamins and minerals that are essential for health, often found in vegetables, fruits, legumes, and whole grains
Millet Group of small, hardy grains such as bajra and ragi
Minced Finely chopped, almost ground, ingredients
Minerals Essential nutrients that the body needs in small amounts, such as calcium, iron, and magnesium
Mock meat Vegetarian substitutes for meat, often made from plant-based ingredients

Moong dal Yellow lentils, derived from the moong bean
Mortar and pestle Traditional tool used for grinding or pounding ingredients
Mughal Prominent historical empire in India, known for its rich cultural, architectural, and artistic contributions, particularly during the 16th to 18th centuries

N

Naggar castle Castle located in Himachal Pradesh
Narali Purnima Festival dedicated to Lord Varuna, the sea god, marking the beginning of the fishing season in Maharashtra
Navalkol Kohlrabi, a bulbous vegetable with a mild, sweet flavour and crunchy texture
Navratri Nine-day festival dedicated to the worship of the Goddess
Neem Tree whose bitter leaves are known for their medicinal properties; often used in Ayurvedic treatments

O

Ole kaju Fresh cashews, typically harvested directly from the cashew tree before being processed and roasted

P

Palghar District in Maharashtra
Pandav Collective term for the five brothers who are the protagonists in the epic *Mahabharata*
Papad Thin, crispy flatbread typically made from lentil flour, rice flour, or gram flour, often deep-fried or roasted
Paryushan Significant Jain festival during which followers fast and pray
Patahjad Autumn season in India
Patni rice Type of rice grown in Maharashtra
Peanuts Groundnuts, commonly used in snacks and chutneys
Phytonutrients Nutrients found in plants, including antioxidants, vitamins, and minerals

Poha Flattened rice, a common breakfast or snack dish
Powdered Ingredients when they are ground into a fine powder
Prasad Food offerings made to deities during religious rituals, which is considered blessed and often shared with devotees afterward
Probiotic Foods that contain live beneficial bacteria that support gut health
Pulses Legumes like lentils, beans, and peas, that are a key source of protein in vegetarian diets
Puran Sweet filling, typically made from jaggery
Puri Deep-fried Indian bread, typically served with vegetable curries

R

Raab Type of porridge made from grains, commonly eaten during the winter season
Ragi Finger millet, typically consumed in summer in India
Rai Mustard seeds, used extensively in tempering as they add a pungent flavour when fried in oil
Raita Curd-based dish, often seasoned with spices and enjoyed as a cooling accompaniment
Rama Seventh incarnation of Lord Vishnu, the preserver god in Hinduism, and the protagonist of the epic *Ramayana*
Red chana Red chickpeas, high in protein and fibre
Ritu Sanskrit term for season, used in the context of the six seasons in the Hindu calendar
Ritusamhara Sanskrit poem by Kalidasa that describes the six seasons of India
Rolling Process of flattening dough into thin sheets
Roop Sanskrit term for appearance
Roti Unleavened flatbread made from wheat flour, a staple dish in India

S

Saar Thin, flavourful soup or broth

Sabudana Tapioca pearls, commonly used in fasting recipes
Sabzi Generic term for vegetable curries or stir-fry
Saffron Highly prized spice derived from the stigma of the crocus flower, used to flavour and colour dishes
Sahyadris Mountain range in Maharashtra, also called the Western Ghats
Saraswati The Hindu goddess of knowledge, music, and wisdom
Sardi Cold or winter season in India
Semolina Coarser form of wheat flour, also known as rava
Sendha namak Rock salt, typically used during fasting periods or when preparing food for special religious occasions as it is considered purer than regular table salt
Sharad Navratri Second of the two major Navratri festivals, celebrated in autumn
Sheetla Ashtami (Basoda) Religious observance dedicated to Goddess Sheetla, who is believed to ward off heat-borne diseases, such as smallpox
Sheng Marathi term for peanuts
Sherbet Sweet, flavoured drink made from fruits, sugar, and spices
Shewaga Drumsticks, also known as moringa
Shewla Wild vegetable that grows just before the rains
Shia Ismaili Branch of the Ismaili Muslim community
Shravan Holy month in the Hindu calendar, often associated with fasting, prayers, and the consumption of light food
Sindh Region in Pakistan
Soaking Process where ingredients are soaked in water to reduce cooking time and improve texture
Sonave Small, tribal village in the Palghar district of Maharashtra
Sookhi lal mirch Dried red chilli peppers, often used whole
Spiti Valley High-altitude region in Himachal Pradesh
Steamer Kitchen appliance used for cooking food in steam

Steaming plate Plate used inside a steamer to cook food

T

Tablescaping Art of decorating a dining table to enhance the dining experience
Tabo Monastery Monastery in Himachal Pradesh
Tadka Process of tempering spices in hot oil or ghee to release their flavours
Tawa Flat, round pan used for cooking flatbreads like rotis, parathas, and dosas, as well as for shallow frying
Tej patta Bay leaves, commonly used whole to add aromatic flavour during tempering and removed before serving
Thangka School Style of traditional Tibetan Buddhist painting that depicts religious subjects
The Food and Agriculture Organization (FAO) of the United Nations International organization that works to eliminate hunger, food insecurity, and malnutrition
Til Sesame seeds
Toor dal Pigeon peas, a type of lentil that is a staple in Indian cuisine
Tulsi Vivah Religious ceremony in Hinduism dedicated to the marriage of Goddess Tulsi to Lord Vishnu, usually observed during the month of Kartika

U

Ukad Marathi term meaning boiled
Upaay Hindi word for remedy or solution
Upvasa Sanskrit term for fasting, a practice where individuals refrain from eating food for a specific period; often observed during religious festivals
Upvasache Foods specifically made for fasting
Urad dal Black gram, a type of lentil
Usal Traditional Maharashtrian bean curry

V

Vaal Hyacinth beans, a type of legume, used to prepare usal (bean curry) or added to dals and vegetable dishes
Vangi Brinjal or eggplant
Vari tandul Barnyard millet, also referred to as sama rice, often used during fasting periods
Variyali Fennel seeds, used as a spice in cooking or as a mouth freshener after meals
Vasant Spring, the season that follows winter and precedes summer in the Indian calendar
Vasant Panchami Hindu festival that marks the arrival of spring and is dedicated to Goddess Saraswati, the goddess of wisdom
Vatane Dried green peas, added to vegetable curries or rice for texture
Vishnu One of the principal deities in Hinduism, considered the preserver of the universe
Vitamins Essential organic compounds required by the body in small amounts for proper metabolism

W

Wadis and wadas Small, bite-sized and large fritters, served as snacks or appetizers
Western coast Coastal region of India, including Maharashtra, Goa, and Gujarat
Western Ghats Mountain range running parallel to the western coast of India
White corn Indigenous variety of corn in India, known for its neutral taste
White pumpkin Also known as ash gourd or winter melon; known for its mild flavour and high water content
Wild vegetables Locally foraged greens that grow naturally without cultivation or care

Y

Yogi Practitioner of yoga, often associated with spiritual practice

Index

A

Aam (mango)
  Aam ras and puri 123
  Mango milkshake 100
  Mango pickle 207
Aliv (garden cress seeds) 205
  Aliv laddoo 205
Almond 126, 149, 170, 223
  Banana halwa 126
  Ragi laddoo 149
  Narali bhaat 170
  White pumpkin halwa 223
Alu (colocasia leaf) 179
  Alu wadi 179
Amaranth seed 206
Ambadi (roselle)
  Ambadi bhaji 180
Ambe dal 219
Amboli 212
Amla (Indian gooseberry) 47
  Amla–ginger sherbet 47
Asafoetida 67, 68, 104, 105, 111, 114, 124, 146, 163, 166, 175, 180, 203, 207, 210, 219, 220, 228

B

Bajra flour 59, 64
  Bajra–green lahasun laddoo 64
  Bajra raab 59
Banana
  Banana halwa 126
  Banana, raw 206
  Banana, ripe 126
  Banana flower 220
  Banana flower sabzi 220
Barnyard millet 166, 206
Bay leaf (tej patta) 71
Bengal gram, split 68, 152, 154, 212, 219
Besan (gram flour) 51, 179, 214, 229
  Besan cheela 229
Bhajani flour 60, 61, 206
Bhakri 215
Bhogichi bhaji 67
Black gram 60, 212
Black chickpea (kala chana) 60
Black gram 212
Black peppercorns 159
Black salt (kala namak) 111, 146

Bottle gourd 114, 229
  Lauki sabzi, jowar roti with ghee, and peanut chutney 114
Brinjal 57, 67
Buttermilk 101, 203, 220, 226

C

Cardamom 59, 149, 168, 170, 223, 224
Carrot 67
Cashew 68, 124, 126, 149, 163, 170, 223, 226
Chana
  Hara chana (green chickpea) 67
Chana dal 68, 152, 154, 212, 219
  Ambe dal 219
  Bengal gram, split 68, 152, 154, 212, 219
Chhole (chickpea) 71
Chickpea 60, 67, 71
Chilli
  Green chilli 51, 52, 53, 68, 101, 104, 105, 114, 118, 152, 166, 203, 206, 219, 220, 229
  Red chilli, dried 57, 154, 180, 206
  Red chilli, powder 53, 57, 61, 67, 71, 111, 124, 127, 163, 175, 179, 180, 207, 210, 212, 214, 220, 228
  Red chilli, whole 57, 154, 180, 206, 219
  Kashmiri red chilli powder 105, 114, 207
Chivda 68
Churmura (puffed rice) 68
Clove 170
Coconut 65
  Coconut, fresh 52, 53, 67, 104, 114, 118, 124, 126, 127, 152, 154, 159, 163, 168, 170, 175, 180, 205, 210, 219, 220, 224, 228
  Coconut milk 118, 124, 159
  Coconut, dry 48, 68
Colocasia leaf 179
Coriander
  Coriander, fresh 51, 152, 228
  Coriander leaf, fresh 114, 118, 163, 214, 219
  Coriander powder 53, 71, 179, 210, 228

  Coriander seed 60, 212
  Sprig of fresh coriander 124, 229
Corn 159
  White corn in khadi and rice 159
Cream 60
Cumin
  Cumin powder 179, 228
  Cumin seed 60, 111, 114, 118, 127, 152, 154, 159, 166, 203, 206, 219
Curd 101, 105, 109, 111, 126, 161, 163, 212, 216, 217, 229
  Curd culture 60
  Curd rice and lemon pickle 105
  Dahi poha 101
Curry 14, 42, 74, 89, 114, 124, 141, 142, 166, 175
Curry leaf 57, 67, 68, 105, 127, 154, 166, 203, 210, 214, 219
  Curry leaves chutney 154

D

Dahi (curd) 101, 105, 111, 163, 212, 226, 229
  Dahi poha 101
Dal
  Ambe dal 219
  Black gram 60
  Bengal gram, split 68, 152, 154, 212, 219
  Chana dal 53, 212
  Dal and bhaat 210
  Green chickpea 67
  Green gram 60
  Green gram, split 111
  Green toor dal (green pigeon pea, split) 67
  Moong dal (green gram) 60
  Toor dal (yellow split pea) 180, 210
  Urad dal 60, 212
Date 111, 149
Danyachi amti and vari
  tandul 166
Dhana jiru (spice mix of coriander and cumin seed) 163
Dhaniya (coriander, coriander seed)
  Dhaniya, fresh 51, 152, 228
  Dhaniya leaf, fresh 114, 118, 163, 214, 219
  Dhaniya powder 53, 71, 179, 210, 228

Dhaniya seed 60, 212
  Sprig of fresh dhaniya 124, 229
Dough 123, 168
Dragon stalk yam 175
Dried green pea 57
Dried red chilli 57, 154, 180, 206, 219
Drumstick 53, 67, 159
Dry coconut 48, 68
Dry fruit 130

E
Elaichi (cardamom)
  Elaichi powder 59, 149, 168, 170, 223, 224

F
Fennel seed 99
Fenugreek seed 207, 212
Field bean 127
Flattened rice 68, 101
Flour
  Bajra flour 59, 64
  Besan flour 51, 179, 214, 229
  Bhajani flour 60, 61, 206
  Gram flour (besan flour) 51, 179, 214, 229
  Jowar flour 60, 115
  Ragi flour 60, 130, 149
  Rice flour 51, 163, 168, 179, 215
  Wheat flour 123
Fresh cashews (ole kaju) 124
Fresh coconut 52, 53, 67, 104, 114, 118, 124, 126, 127, 152, 154, 159, 163, 168, 170, 175, 180, 205, 210, 219, 220, 224, 228
Fresh coconut milk 124
Fresh coriander 51, 124, 152, 228, 229
Fresh coriander leaf 114, 118, 163, 214, 219
Fresh ginger 49, 53, 150, 217
Fruit
  Dry fruit 130
  Khajoor 111, 149
  Mango, raw 207, 219
  Mango, ripe 100, 123
Full-fat milk 101, 226

G
Garam masala 53, 175
Garden cress seed 205

Garlic 51, 114, 118, 127, 152, 175, 180, 212, 214
  Green lahasun (green garlic) 64
Ghee 48, 59, 64, 111, 114, 126, 146, 149, 159, 163, 166, 168, 170, 203, 205, 206, 212, 224
Ginger
  Ginger, fresh 47, 51, 118, 152, 229
  Ginger–garlic paste 53, 71
  Ginger powder 59
Goda masala 57, 67, 111, 124, 163, 220
Gourd
  Bottle gourd 114, 229
  Spiny gourd 228
Green chilli 51, 52, 53, 68, 101, 104, 105, 114, 118, 152, 166, 203, 206, 219, 220, 229
Gram flour 51, 179, 214, 229
Grated coconut, fresh 52, 53, 67, 104, 114, 118, 124, 126, 127, 152, 154, 159, 163, 168, 170, 175, 180, 205, 210, 219, 220, 224, 228
Green chickpea 67
Green garlic 64
Green gram 60
Green pigeon split pea 67
Green toor dal (green pigeon split pea) 67
Green pea 124

H
Haldi (turmeric powder) 51, 53, 57, 61, 67, 68, 111, 124, 127, 163, 175, 179, 180, 207, 210, 212, 214, 219, 220, 228
Halwa
  Banana halwa 126
  White pumpkin halwa 223
Hara chana (green chickpea) 67
Hing (asafoetida) 67, 68, 104, 105, 111, 114, 124, 146, 163, 166, 175, 180, 203, 207, 210, 219, 220, 228
Horse gram (kulith) 203

I
Indian gooseberry (amla) 47
  Amla–ginger sherbet 47

J
Jaggery 48, 59, 67, 124, 126, 130, 149, 166, 168, 170, 179, 180, 205, 220
Jaman (curd culture) 60
Jaiphal (nutmeg)
  Jaiphal powder 48, 126, 130, 149, 168, 170, 205, 223, 226
Jeera (cumin seed and powder)
  Jeera powder 179, 228
  Jeera seed 60, 111, 114, 118, 127, 152, 154, 159, 166, 203, 206, 219
Jowar flour 115

K
Kaju (cashew)
  Ole kaju usal 124
Kala chana (black chickpea) 60
Kala namak (black salt) 111, 146
Kali mirch (black peppercorns) 159
Kantola vegetable 228
Kashmiri lal mirch (Kashmiri red chilli powder) 105, 114, 207
Kashmiri red chilli powder (Kashmiri lal mirch) 105, 114, 207
Kesar (saffron strands) 168, 226
Khadi shakkar (unrefined sugar) 99
Khajoor (date) 149
Khichdi and date raita 111
Kohlrabi 52
Kokum 210
  Kokum agal (extract) 118
  Kokum, dried 163, 166
  Kokum saar 118
  Kokum water 163
Kothimbir (fresh coriander) 51
  Kothimbir wadi 51
Kulith (horse gram) 203
  Kulith kalan 203

L
Laddoo 64, 149, 205, 224
  Aliv 205
  Bajra–green lahasun 64
  Ragi 149
  Rava–nariyal 224
  Til gul 48
Lahasun, green 64

Lal mirch (red chilli powder) 53, 57,
   61, 67, 71, 111, 124, 127, 163,
   175, 179, 180, 207, 210, 212,
   214, 220, 228
Lal mirch, Kashmiri 105, 114, 207
   Lal mirch, sookhi (red chilli, dried)
      57, 154, 180, 206, 219
Lauki (bottle gourd) 114, 229
   Lauki sabzi, jowar roiti with ghee,
      and peanut chutney 114
Laung (clove) 170
Leaf
   Colocasia 155
   Curry 57, 67, 68, 105, 127, 154,
      166, 203, 210, 214, 219
Lemon 105
   Lemon juice 47, 104
   Lemon pickle 105
   Lemon slices 47
Loni 60

M

Maharashtrian spice mix (goda
   masala) 57, 67, 111, 124, 163,
   220
Mango
   Aam ras and puri 123
   Mango, green, raw 207, 219
   Mango milkshake 100
   Mango pickle 207
Masala
   Dhaniya powder (coriander) 53,
      71, 179, 210, 228
   Elaichi powder 59, 149, 168, 170,
      223, 224
   Garam masala 53, 175
   Goda masala 57, 67, 111, 124,
      163, 220
   Haldi masala 51, 53, 57, 61, 67, 68,
      111, 124, 127, 163, 175, 179, 180,
      207, 210, 212, 214, 219, 220, 228
   Hing powder (asafoetida) 47, 67,
      68, 104, 105, 111, 114, 124,
      146, 163, 166, 175, 180, 203,
      207, 210, 219, 220, 228
   Jaiphal powder 48, 126, 130, 149,
      168, 170, 205, 223, 226
   Jeera powder (cumin powder)
      179, 228
   Kashmiri lal mirch (Kashmiri red
      chilli powder) 105, 114, 207

Lal mirch powder 53, 57, 61, 67,
   71, 111, 124, 127, 163, 179,
   180, 207, 210, 212, 214, 220,
   228
Nutmeg powder 48, 126, 130,
   149, 168, 170, 205, 223, 226
Spice mix of coriander and cumin
   seed 163
Turmeric powder 51, 53, 55, 58,
   65, 66, 105, 109, 122, 155, 161,
   180, 207, 208, 212, 214, 223,
   228
Makai (corn) 159
Malai (cream) 60
Masala bhaat and yam kaap 163
Methi (fenugreek seed) 207, 212
Milk 59, 100, 101, 130, 168, 205, 226
   Full-fat milk 101, 226
Moong dal (green gram) 60,
   111
Mustard seed (rai seed) 52, 57, 67,
   68, 104, 105, 111, 118, 124, 126,
   127, 163, 175, 179, 180, 207, 210,
   214, 219, 220, 228
Mustard seed, powdered 207

N

Narali bhaat 170
Nariyal (fresh coconut) 224
   Nariyal laddoo 224
Navalkol (kohlrabi) 52
   Navalkol koshimbir 52
Nutmeg powder 48, 126, 130,
   149, 168, 170, 205, 223, 226

O

Oil 51, 52, 53, 57, 61, 64, 67, 68, 71,
   104, 105, 114, 115, 118, 123, 124,
   127, 152, 154, 163, 175, 179, 180,
   207, 210, 214, 219, 220, 228, 229
   Ghee 48, 59, 64, 111, 114, 115,
      126, 146, 149, 159, 163, 166,
      168, 170, 203, 205, 206, 212,
      224
   Mustard oil 207
   Peanut oil 64
   Sesame oil 64
Onion 53, 61, 71, 104, 127, 175,
   214, 228
   White onion 104
   White onion koshimbir 104

P

Peanut 48, 52, 53, 67, 68, 104, 114,
   152, 159, 166, 180, 206, 220
   Peanut chutney 114
   Peanut, crushed 52
   Peanut oil 64
   Peanut, powdered 53, 104, 114,
      152, 206
   Peanut, roasted 68
Pearl millet (bajra) 59, 64
Pea 57, 124, 163
   Green pea 124
   Green pea, dried 57
Pickle
   Lemon 105
   Mango 207
Pistachio 126, 226
Pithla and bhakri 214
Pithla 214
Poha (flattened rice) 68, 101
Potato 53, 67, 152
Puffed rice (churmura) 68
Pumpkin 206, 223, 229
   Red pumpkin 206, 229
   White pumpkin 223
   White pumpkin halwa 223
Puran 168

R

Ragi
   Ragi flour 60, 130, 149
   Ragi kheer 130
   Ragi laddoo 149
Rai
   Powder 207
   Seed (mustard seed) 52, 57, 67,
      68, 104, 105, 111, 118, 124,
      126, 127, 163, 175, 179, 180,
      207, 210, 214, 219, 220, 228
Raisin 223, 224
Rava (semolina) 224
   Rava–nariyal laddoo 224
Red chilli powder
   Kashmiri lal mirch (Kashmiri red
      chilli powder) 105, 114, 207

Red chilli powder 53, 57, 61, 67, 71, 111, 124, 127, 163, 179, 180, 207, 210, 212, 214, 220, 228
Red pumpkin 206, 229
Rice
   Churmura rice 68
   Flattened rice (poha) 68, 101
   Khichdi and date raita 111
   Rice 57, 60, 111, 146, 159, 163, 170, 180, 212
   Rice flour 51, 163, 168, 179, 215
   Rice pej 146
   Small-grain rice 105
Rice pej 146
Roasted sesame seed (tilkut) 67
Rock salt 47, 111, 207
   Black salt (kala namak) 111, 146
   Sea salt 105
Roselle leaf 180
Roti
   Bhakri 215
   Thalipeeth 61, 206

S

Sabudana (tapioca pearls) 152, 206
   Sabudana wada and chutney 152
Saffron strands 168, 226
Salt 51, 52, 53, 57, 61, 64, 67, 68, 71, 101, 104, 114, 118, 123, 124, 127, 130, 152, 154, 159, 163, 166, 168, 175, 179, 180, 203, 206, 210, 212, 214, 215, 219, 220, 228, 229
   Rock salt 47, 111, 207
   Black salt (kala namak) 111, 146
   Sea salt 105
   Sendha namak 47, 111, 207
Sea salt 105
Seed
   Amaranth 206
   Coriander seed 60, 212
   Cumin seed 60, 111, 114, 118, 127, 152, 154, 159, 166, 203, 206, 219
   Fennel seed 99
   Fenugreek seed 207, 212
   Mustard seed 52, 57, 67, 68, 104, 105, 111, 118, 124, 126, 127, 163, 175, 179, 180, 207, 210, 214, 219, 220, 228

Mustard seed, powdered 207
Sesame seed 35, 48, 51, 67, 68, 154, 179
Semolina 123, 163, 224, 229
Sendha namak (rock salt) 47, 111, 207
Sesame seed 48, 51, 68, 154, 179
Shakkar (unrefined sugar) 99
Sheng amti 53
Shewaga (drumsticks) 53, 67, 159
Shewla (dragon stalk yam) 175
Shewla bhaji 175
Shrikhand 226
Sookhi lal mirch (red chilli, dried) 57, 154, 180, 206, 219
Spice mix of coriander and cumin seed 163
Spiny gourd 228
Split Bengal gram 68, 152, 154, 212, 219
Split chickpea 150, 212
Split green gram (moong dal) 111
Split yellow pea (toor dal) 180
Sugar 47, 68, 99, 104, 105, 114, 118, 123, 152, 203, 219, 223, 224, 228
   Powdered 226
   Unrefined (shakkar) 99

T

Tamarind extract 179
Tapioca pearls (sabudana) 152, 206
Tea powder 71
Tej patta (bay leaf) 71
Thalipeeth 61, 206
   Thalipeeth and loni 60
Til (sesame seed) 48, 51, 68, 154, 179
   Til gul 48
Tilkut (roasted sesame seed) 67
Tomato 53, 67, 71, 127
Toor dal (yellow pea, split) 180, 228
   Dal and bhaat 210
Turmeric powder 51, 53, 57, 61, 67, 68, 111, 124, 127, 163, 175, 179, 180, 207, 210, 212, 214, 219, 220, 228

U

Ukad (dough) 166
   Ukadiche modak 168
Unrefined sugar 99

Upvasache thalipeeth 206
Urad dal (black gram) 60, 212

V

Vaal (field bean) 127
   Vaal usal 127
Vangi (brinjal) 57
   Vangi bhaat 57
Vari rice (barnyard millet) 166, 206
   Vari tandul 166
Variyali (fennel seeds) 99
   Variyali sherbet 99
Vatane (green pea, dried) 57

W

Wheat flour 123
White corn in kadhi and rice 159
White onion 104
   White onion koshimbir 104
White pumpkin 223
   White pumpkin halwa 223
Whole urad dal (black gram) 60, 212

Y

Yam 159, 163
   Yam kaap 163
Yellow pea, split 180

Acknowledgments

About the author

Rujuta Diwekar is India's leading public health advocate and one of the most followed nutritionists globally. Her books have sold more than 1.5 million copies and have been translated into seven languages. With her clear and simple message to eat local, seasonal, and traditional foods, she has redefined the discourse on health and wellness – nudging it away from diet trends and towards the sustainable well-being of people and the planet.

Author's acknowledgments

From the time I wrote *Don't Lose Your Mind, Lose Your Weight*, I have been flooded with offers to write a recipe book. I was advised that whenever a diet book becomes a bestseller, it is almost always followed by a recipe book. That insight was enough to serve as a strong deterrent for me. For over 15 years, I avoided recipes because I did not want any one approach to cooking or cuisine to become the way to lose weight or stay healthy. Had it not been for Aparna – her prudence, perseverance, and passion – I never would have committed to writing this book, let alone finishing it. Aparna, this book is for you. And through you, for every woman who pours her heart into everything she touches. Thank you for getting me to do this.

This book is my attempt to share timeless recipes that I have cooked in my kitchen, and with new fervour since the lockdown. Cooking has become a journey of discovery, one that has deepened my appreciation for the wisdom of women, their ability to source ingredients, and bring them together in meaningful dishes and delicacies. May their wisdom and kindness inspire your own kitchen and touch your heart. And may your stomach and soul always be nourished.

None of this would have been possible without the incredible team at DK, led by Aparna. Vatsal, who spent many hours talking with me and helped put together the book for me. Neha, Chitra, and Bhavika, who worked tirelessly on this project and truly made it their own.

A special thank you to my team back in the office, especially Jinal, Naghma, Ghazal, and GP, who generously set aside their own schedules to accommodate mine. Your support made all the difference.

And to my mother, without whom I would never have understood that cooking is not just a craft, but the ultimate act of feminism and freedom. Your influence shaped everything.

A woman who cooks and nourishes herself will always have a beautiful life and a meal to share with those she loves and calls her own.

Publisher's acknowledgments

The publisher would like to thank Avanika, Pranay Mathur, Ankita Gupta, and Khushi Seth for editorial support; Devika Awasthi for design support; Sushmita Choudhury for proofreading; Tarun Khanna for indexing; Adhyayan Sahay for recipe testing; Raman Panwar and Umesh Singh Rawat for technical support; Samrajkumar S for picture credits; Harish Aggarwal and Suhita Dharamjit for support in jacket design; Bhavika Mathur, Vatsal Verma, and Neha Ahuja Chowdhry for providing props; and Aparna Sharma for graciously offering her space for photography.

Publisher's note

Every effort has been made to ensure that the information contained in this book is complete and accurate. However, neither the publisher nor the author are engaged in rendering professional advice or services to the individual reader. Professional medical advice should be obtained on personal health matters. Neither the publisher nor the author accept any legal responsibility for any personal injury or other damage or loss arising from the use or misuse of the information and advice in this book.

Disclaimer: Every effort has been made to acknowledge those individuals, organizations, and corporations that have helped with this book and to trace copyright holders. DK apologizes in advance if any omission has occurred. If an omission does come to light, DK will be pleased to insert the appropriate acknowledgment in subsequent editions of the book.

The publisher would like to thank the following for their kind permission to reproduce their photographs: (Key: a-above; b-below/bottom; c-centre; f-far; l-left; r-right; t-top)

2 Anamika Singh. 4-5 Dreamstime.com: Lemusique. Shutterstock.com: Artology Namaha (b). 6-7 Shutterstock.com: Artology Namaha (b). 9 Dreamstime.com: Sameer Marathe (bc). 10-25 Dreamstime.com: Sameer Marathe (t). 12 Rujuta Diwekar. 12-13 Rujuta Diwekar: (c). 15 Rujuta Diwekar. 18-19 Rujuta Diwekar: (c). 22-23 Anamika Singh. 24 Rujuta Diwekar. 24-25 Rujuta Diwekar: (c). 26-27 Anamika Singh. 29 Dreamstime.com: Iuliia Selina (bc). 30-31 Rujuta Diwekar. 31-180 Dreamstime.com: Iuliia Selina (t). 33 Rujuta Diwekar. 34 Dreamstime.com: Chernetskaya (l). 34-35 Alamy Stock Photo: Zoonar GmbH / Olena Yemchuk (bc). Shutterstock.com: Ratheep R (c). 36 Rujuta Diwekar. 37 Rujuta Diwekar. 38-39 Rujuta Diwekar. 40-41 Rujuta Diwekar: (c). 42 Rujuta Diwekar. 43 Rujuta Diwekar. 45 Depositphotos Inc: Lyhoanglong (tl). Shutterstock.com: Md. Noor Mahbub Alam (tr).

62-64 Dreamstime.com: Lemusique. 62-63 Shutterstock.com: Artology Namaha (b). 73 Dreamstime.com: Iuliia Selina (cb). 74-75 Anamika Singh. 75 Rujuta Diwekar. 78-79 Rujuta Diwekar: (c). 80-81 Rujuta Diwekar. 82-83 Dreamstime.com: Blanscape (bc); Zbynek Pospisil (c). 83 Shutterstock.com: ShivajiOrbit (r). 84 Rujuta Diwekar. 86 Rujuta Diwekar. 89 Rujuta Diwekar. 91 Rujuta Diwekar. 94-95 Rujuta Diwekar. 108-109 Dreamstime.com: Lemusique. Shutterstock.com: Yulianas (b). 111 Dreamstime.com: Lemusique. 112-115 Dreamstime.com: Lemusique. 112-113 Shutterstock.com: Yulianas (bc). 120-121 Dreamstime.com: Lemusique. Shutterstock.com: Yulianas (b). 123 Dreamstime.com: Lemusique. 128-130 Dreamstime.com: Lemusique. 128-129 Shutterstock.com: Yulianas (b). 133 Dreamstime.com: Iuliia Selina (cb). 136 Rujuta Diwekar. 136-137 Rujuta Diwekar: (bc). 140-141 Dreamstime.com: Buppha Wuttifery (ca). 150-152 Dreamstime.com: Lemusique. 150-151 Shutterstock.com: Artology Namaha (b). 156-157 Dreamstime.com: Lemusique. Shutterstock.com: Artology Namaha (b). 159-161 Dreamstime.com: Lemusique. 160-161 Shutterstock.com: Artology Namaha (b). 163-166 Dreamstime.com: Lemusique. 164-165 Shutterstock.com: Artology Namaha (b). 172-173 Dreamstime.com: Lemusique. Shutterstock.com: Artology Namaha (b). 175-177 Dreamstime.com: Lemusique. 176-177 Shutterstock.com: Artology Namaha (b). 179 Dreamstime.com: Lemusique. 183 Dreamstime.com: Sameer Marathe (c). 184-185 Rujuta Diwekar. 185-229 Dreamstime.com: Sameer Marathe (t). 187 Rujuta Diwekar. 188 Rujuta Diwekar. 190 Rujuta Diwekar. 196 Rujuta Diwekar. 196-197 Rujuta Diwekar: (c). 198-199 Rujuta Diwekar: (ca). 199 Rujuta Diwekar: (cla, cra). 200 Rujuta Diwekar. 200-201 Rujuta Diwekar: (c). 216-217 Dreamstime.com: Lemusique. Shutterstock.com: Artology Namaha (b). 219 Dreamstime.com: Lemusique

Senior Editor Vatsal Verma
Senior Art Editor Bhavika Mathur
Jacket Designer Neha Ahuja Chowdhry
Pre-production Designer Anurag Trivedi
Pre-production Image Editor Syed Md Farhan
Pre-production Coordinator Tarun Sharma
Pre-Production Manager Balwant Singh
Pre-production Image Manager Pankaj Sharma
Managing Editor Chitra Subramanyam
Managing Art Editor Neha Ahuja Chowdhry
Consulting Publisher Aparna Sharma

Food and prop styling Bhavika Mathur, Vatsal Verma
Photography Aarish Bhathena
Recipe prep Sonal Garg, Shwetha Shashikant Wagh

First published in Great Britain in 2025 by
Dorling Kindersley Limited
20 Vauxhall Bridge Road,
London SW1V 2SA

The authorised representative in the EEA is
Dorling Kindersley Verlag GmbH. Arnulfstr. 124,
80636 Munich, Germany

Text copyright © 2025 Rujuta Diwekar
Copyright © 2025 Dorling Kindersley Limited
A Penguin Random House Company
10 9 8 7 6 5 4 3 2 1
001–336431–July/2025

All rights reserved. No part of this publication may be reproduced, stored in or introduced into a retrieval system, or transmitted, in any form, or by any means (electronic, mechanical, photocopying, recording, or otherwise), without the prior written permission of the copyright owner.
DK values and supports copyright. Thank you for respecting intellectual property laws by not reproducing, scanning or distributing any part of this publication by any means without permission. By purchasing an authorised edition, you are supporting writers and artists and enabling DK to continue to publish books that inform and inspire readers. No part of this publication may be used or reproduced in any manner for the purpose of training artificial intelligence technologies or systems. In accordance with Article 4(3) of the DSM Directive 2019/790, DK expressly reserves this work from the text and data mining exception.

A CIP catalogue record for this book
is available from the British Library.
ISBN: 978-0-2416-3015-0

Printed and bound in China

www.dk.com